SWAMI FOR PRECEDENT

A 7 Step Plan to Heal the Body Politic and Cure Electile Dysfunction

BY SWAMI BEYONDANANDA

ILLUSTRATED BY BRIAN NARELLE

WakeUpLaughing Press, Santa Rosa, California

Swami for Precedent, A 7 Step Plan to Heal the Body Politic and Cure Electile Dysfunction, by Swami Beyondananda.

Published by
WakeUpLaughing Press
400 W. Third St., Suite D-144
Santa Rosa, CA 95401
(707) 525-0778

Cover and interior design by Lightbourne, Inc.
www.lightbourne.com

Illustrations by Brian Narelle
www.narellecreative.com

Cover photo of Swami by Trudy Bhaerman
Cover photo of White House by www.gettyimages.com

ISBN 0-9755983-0-9

Printed in the United States of America.
10   9   8   7   6   5   4   3   2   1

★ ★ ★ ★ ★ ★ ★ ★ ★ ★ ★ ★ ACKNOWLEDGMENTS

I would like to thank all of those who supported this project with their good wishes, their good ideas, their encouragement, and their financial support. Thanks to all of you who had the confidence to pre-buy books!

Specifically, thank you Michael Mears for giving me the seed of this idea two years ago, and Steve Wagner for being an encouraging force throughout. Thanks to our publicists, John Raatz and David Langer of the Visioneering Group for support, encouragement and good thinking. Thanks to Allison, Bob and Shannon at Lightbourne for your awesome design of this book, to my wife Trudy for the cover photo, and of course Brian Narelle for his illustrations that take the Swami's humor to another level.

Thanks to the three Jims — Jim Courtney, Jim Lauria and Jim Wasner — for helping with cash flow when we needed it. Thanks too to Janet Williams, Larry Nisson, Phil and Karen Moore, David Friedland, and Gail and Mike Whitty for providing financial support at key times. Thanks to all of you — and you know who you are — who joined the Right to Laugh Party, who pre-purchased books, and who otherwise put your assets on the line.

Thanks to colleagues Thom Hartmann and Jimmy Langkop, who offered ideas and feedback, and to Stephanie Bruce who did so much of the research. Thanks to our office assistant Annette Toivonen, and Connie Bertlshofer who worked on the dictionary.

I also want to acknowledge Patricia McDade and the staff at the Consulting Alliance, who inspired the larger conversation that made this book possible.

And above all, thank you to my beloved wife and partner, Trudy, for your steadfast devotion, support and inspiration. Thank you, Trudy for your unwavering confidence in this out-of-the-box project, for all your work in creating the infrastructure for success, and — when all is said and done — for being my bright, radiant light at the end of the tunnel.

A Funny Thing Happened on the Way to Enlightenment

By Steve Bhaerman

I've been following Swami Beyondananda for nearly 25 years now. His name flew into my head one evening as I was casting about for a character to bring humor to a new holistic publication I was starting called Pathways. He and I have been stuck together ever since, and I've always been grateful for that life-changing moment when I was struck by enlightening during a brainstorm.

During those days in the early 80s when I and so many others were the "tire-kickers" of various spiritual movements, the Swami was there to set us straight and offer real spiritual perspective: Beware of spiritual teachers and aspirants who cannot laugh at themselves. Avoid self-flagellating practices, programs and diets that diminish the Spirit by focusing only on arbitrary rules. Learn to recognize psycho-spiritual manipulation in the form of "Why did you create this?" Watch out for blatant materialism cloaked in spiritual robes, where inner work is done solely for outer riches.

The "laughorisms" that came through Swami in those early days were mainly reminders to help those who had embarked on the path looking out for "number one" to start looking out for "number two" as well:

> There's a seeker born every minute, and two to take him
>   along the path.
> When you see a sacred cow, milk it for all it's worth.
> Drive your karma, curb your dogma.
> Use mental floss to help prevent truth decay.
> Practice FUNdamentalism, accent on fun.

It was the Swami's success in print that nudged my wife Trudy and I to leave our safe haven in Ann Arbor, Michigan for an extended tour that has lasted about eighteen years now. Along the way, the Swami has softened my New York state of mind, and offered me a chance at a kinder and gentler relationship with my audience that most club comics cannot fathom.

By the mid-90s, I noticed that the spiritual materialism and pathological purity I'd seen in the early days of the "new age" movement had given way to more maturity. Folks once addicted to "positive thinking" began to talk about "the shadow," and those who used to chant for BMWs now were chanting for the happiness of all beings. Swami shifted his mission too, to focus on the healing power of laughter. Swami's book, *Duck Soup for the Soul* and his CD, *Beyondananda and Beyond*, both reflect this focus on laughter as both an ends and a means.

But . . . a funny thing happened on the way to enlightenment.

The election in 2000 became a "selection," and those heady, expansive days of the 1990s — captured by Bill Clinton's campaign theme song from Fleetwood Mac, "Don't Stop Thinking About Tomorrow" — was condensed by a new administration to simply "Stop Thinking." And the replacement Fleetwood Mac tune was, "Tell Me Lies." Then came 9/11. The Democrats' roll-over-and-play-dead act in 2002. The run-up to the Iraqi Horror Picture Show. And all of a sudden, all of the individual enlightenment cultivated over ten or fifteen years was overshadowed by the endarkenment of the unacknowledged shadow. As the Swami put it, "It's hard to live a holistic life in an assaholistic system."

And so the Swami embarked on a new mission — to bring the light of healing laughter and love to the poorly lit corridors of power. Swami even considered running for President. But it became clear that 2004 would be no Pat Paulsen year. There are those who are simply not amused by George Bush, and who were concerned the Swami would take votes from a real candidate. Seriously. Despite the Swami's reassurance that he only planned to take votes from nonvoters ("If all the nonvoters vote for me, I will win in a landslide!"), in the end Swami chose the role of "uncommontator" and the mission of helping America choose a new "precedent."

What the Swami and I discovered in last fall's cross-country tour was the great relief people felt at hearing "the truth" and being able to laugh at it. Everywhere we went — from a conservative community north of San Diego to the Midwest to Florida, and even Texas — audiences told us how encouraged and empowered they were to see so many people laughing in the face of their worst fears about the direction America has been taking.

I recently wrote a "serious" article on what I call the "Not-See Menace." Drawing on oral histories of pre-war Germany, I saw that the enablers for the Nazis were the "Not-Sees" — the average, ordinary people who failed to recognize the potential for evil in their midst. Today, American "Not-Sees" are failing to notice the warning signs of absolute power corrupting absolutely. Those apologists for the prison camp atrocities in Iraq, Afghanistan and Guantanamo, those who look the other way when our current misleaders put themselves above the law, those who fall into line because this is "wartime" (which we've been assured will last indefinitely) are all abdicating the power given to the people in our Declaration of Independence and Constitution. At a time when we've been hearing so much talk about bringing democracy to the world, what tragic irony it would be to lose it here.

You know, sometimes it's just not funny. There's nothing funny about terrorists flying airplanes into buildings, and nothing funny about children dying in our bombing attacks on Afghanistan and Iraq. But in a world where so much dysfunctional insanity is called sane, comedy has the power to be the ultimate weapon of mass deconstruction — particularly if it's done without cynicism. The best comedy milks the sacred cow, and at the same time helps us distinguish it from the profane bull. This is a time when we can use all the distinguished distinctions we can get.

As a former political science major and history teacher, and as someone who's immersed myself in various spiritual teachings and practices, the question I've been asking lately is, "What do we humans do now? How do we apply our spiritual practice and all of those high-minded values to our lives and world?"

And the answer that's come to me is: Wake up! Wake up, everyone. Wake up laughing, and wake up loving!

There is an old Chinese curse — or blessing — that says, "May you live in interesting times." Well, here we are. Who needs reality TV? We ARE reality TV! We have all the love, brilliance, dedication, know-how, courage, devotion we need to take on a worthy challenge: To redirect Space Ship Earth from its frightening course toward Armageddon and Judgment Day to the safer and saner harbors of Disarmageddon and Nonjudgment Day.

It's as simple as Swami's silly yet profound joke: Don't get even, get odd. My hope and prayer for this book is that it helps to trip another circuit, maybe the same circuit that used to flicker in the late great Jimmy Durante's eyes when he would shout, "Stop da music! *Stop da music!"*

The blaring trumpets, the drumbeat of war, it is the same familiar dysfunctional tune we've been marching to for millennia. I say it's high time we the people of the world stopped the old, tired music and changed our tune. We need to lift our heads above the dueling dualities chiding us to "get even," and together choose the odd solutions that recognize our Oneness. This may sound like idealism, but I say it's real-dealism. Like the individual who must make a radical change in lifestyle to heal from a life-threatening illness, we must face the life-threatening conditions on our planet and take the practical steps for healing that will help us survive.

It is not my intention to create unnecessary antagonism with this book. I apologize in advance for anything my Republican or conservative friends might take "poisonally." As the great umpire Bill Klem used to say, "I call 'em as I see 'em." And as I see this one, the Republican Party has been taken over by a cadre that masks cynical greed and anti-life agenda behind the righteousness of the Religious Right. There are those very, very close to the seat of power that believe that since Armageddon is near, why the hell bother cleaning up the environment? I wish that were a joke, but it's not.

And just as we are calling on moderate Muslims to distinguish themselves from the unfun fundamentalist forces that have hijacked their religion, Americans of all political persuasions must stand for transparency and the checks and balances that will keep the dark forces in our own midst from using the very real danger in the world to give themselves unlimited and unchecked power.

Think for a moment about the awesome gift our nation's founders gave us. Drawing from the Enlightenment in Europe and the Iroquois Nations, they offered the truly inspired and

unheard-of idea that we humans are sovereign citizens, not subjects, who voluntarily join to preserve and enhance our commonwealth.

Now, as the Swami will tell you in the following pages, we
need an American Evolution to grow into the ideals that have
been set for us, and to inspire others to do the same. For in this
shrinking world that could definitely use a good shrink, there is
nowhere to run and nowhere to hide from either our destiny —
or the prospect of our demise as a species. And there doesn't seem
to be much middle ground these days.

Maybe we need to be as hawkish and steadfast as the current
regime in declaring our own "pro-life" agenda. Maybe we need to
remind ourselves of the one immutable power in the Universe,
one that each and every one of us has experienced — the power
of Loving Goodness that is bigger than any of the limiting labels
we give it.

May we use the power of loving laughter to open our eyes,
open our hearts and restore the health and vitality in our body
politic. May we use the power of imagination, the most abundant
human resource on the planet, to find unthought-of solutions
that will help us avoid the unthinkable. May we take back our
government and give the world an object lesson in liberty and
democracy. And may we honor all our relations, and the essence
of all our spiritual traditions by trusting that indeed, *right* makes
might and *only love prevails*.

★ CONTENTS

preface **A Funny Thing Happened on
the Way to Enlightenment** ★ *vii*

introduction **It's Time for a New Precedent** ★ *xv*

One **Let's Elect Ourselves!** ★ *1*
Time to Act Like Citizens, Not Subjects
*"Government of the people, by the people,
for the people . . . people — hey, that's us!"*

Two **Improve Reality!** ★ *23*
From Original Sin to Humanifest Destiny
*"Why don't we go for heaven on Earth —
just for the hell of it?"*

Three **Pray It Forward** ★ *43*
And Practice Supply-Side Spirituality
*"We're not here to earn God's love,
we're here to spend it."*

Four **Tell-A-Vision** ★ *67*
And Change the Programming for Good
*"If you don't like the current programming,
turn off your TV and tell a vision instead."*

Five **Invest in A-Bun-Dance, Not Scare-City** ★ *91*
How to Feed Two Birds With One Scone, and
Make the Commonwealth Uncommonly Wealthy
*"Let's put our money into goods and
services instead of bads and disservices."*

Six **Revitalize the Body Politic** ✶ *115*
How to Exercise Our Rights and
Re-Constitute the Constitution
*"Time to pump ironies and
do free press presses."*

Seven **Don't Get Even, Get Odd!** ✶ *141*
Politics As Unusual
*"Forget about getting even. If the Law of
Karma is right, odds are it will all even
out in the end anyway."*

Swami's Dictionary ✶ *165*
Resources & Recourses ✶ *181*

It's Time for a New Precedent!

You may have the heard the rumor circulating — and I know it was circulating because I started it myself — that I was running for President. Now, you might be saying, "A comedian for President? Ha! Don't make me laugh!" Well, many Americans agree there is definitely something funny going on, so why *not* a comedian?

My inner voice told me to run for President, or so I thought. Now my inner voice, like my outer voice, speaks with a slight East Indian accent, and is sometimes hard to understand. So I replayed my inner messages, and what do you know? It said, "Swami, we need a new *precedent.*"

Yes, in these unprecedented times what we really need to do is set a new precedent, and a new President will follow. Because if we only do things the way we've always done them, we'll only get what we've always gotten. Even a rat will stop pulling the lever when there's no more cheese and, as an optimystic, I have to believe we humans are smarter than rats.

The Body Politic is One Sick Puppy

Now I've had my finger on the pulse of the body politic, and I have good news. We still have a pulse. Barely. Because the body politic has suffered some serious power seizures, and our Constitution has been weakened. Thanks to the steady diet of junk food the media has been feeding us, the body politic has become a bloated couch potato behind a remote. Meanwhile, the government is on steroids.

If Thomas Jefferson were alive today, do you know what he'd say? First thing he'd say is, "Boy do I feel old!" But then he'd say, the government serves at the pleasure of the people, and a lot of us aren't being served. He'd say we've ended up with some self-serving servants. They're serving themselves first, their cronies second, and we the people are picking up the tab. Jefferson would say, "Let's fire those servants!"

And he'd be outraged at the things our government is hiding from us. He'd be asking, how come they get to play "I've Got a Secret," and we're forced "To Tell the Truth"? He'd say, "Talk about games governments play. They're playing 'Wheel of Fortune', and they've left us in 'Jeopardy'."

Did you know that a trillion dollars…that's $1,000,000,000,000, a truly numbing number . . . a trillion dollars disappeared from the Defense Department treasury a couple of years ago. Poof. Just like that. Now, maybe I just missed it, but I didn't see that story on "Unsolved Mysteries", did you? The "Trillion Dollar Question", now there's a reality show I would watch.

Jefferson, radical that he was, would be saying, "Forget the air-line passengers. Let's strip search the government!"

One Nation, Under Guard

The body politic is indeed in serious condition, thanks to seri-ousness caused not just by terrorism but by anti-terrorism as well. I don't know which one is more terrifying, although I will say this. The war on terror has made our lives simpler. They've taken the Bill of Rights and they've boiled it down to just one. You have the right to remain silent. And like every other war, it's led to great techno-logical advances. In the early 1960s, President John F. Kennedy declared that he would have a man on the moon by the end of that decade. And look how far we've come. Thanks to the so-called Patriot Act, George Bush can have someone on Uranus by the end of the week. Yes, we can proudly say we are "One nation, under guard."

Meanwhile, the Irony Curtain Has Come Down

Sadly, 2003 was the year the Irony Curtain descended over America — the invisible wall of impropaganda they put up to separate people from the truth. And to make sure that Americans didn't "get smart" enough to see through to the truth, a Cone of Silence came down as well, and far too many well-known people became cone heads and allowed themselves to be silenced. So when Michael Moore broke through the soundless barrier at the Academy Awards it was a moment of truth in a year that was short on truthful moments.

True, this is a dangerous world and, while Mr. Cheney can hide himself in some undisclosed location, Mr. Bush has to make a public appearance from time to time, and must be protected at all costs . . . from free speech. So to make sure that criticism of his policies doesn't become massive enough to reach critical mass, protestors are now cordoned off behind barbed wire in what are called . . . and I am not making this up, because comic irony has nothing on tragic irony . . . "Free Speech Zones." This insures that Americans still have the right to speak freely — as long as no one can hear them. Or maybe it's that free speech has become so endangered, it needs to be protected behind barbed wire. Which leads us to the philosophical question, "If a speech falls freely in the forest and there is no one there to hear, is it still free speech?"

Now you would think they'd leave Orwell enough alone, but no. Remember, "War is Peace"? Well, in case you don't, the concept is back with a vengeance. Isn't that why we've been fighting in Iraq, to insure peace? To paraphrase Dick Cheney, "We will continue fighting our war for peace, even if it takes FOREVER!"

At this writing, the War on Iraq is just over a year old, and it has cost us over $107 billion. That comes out to $293,150,685 a day! Do the math. And if you find the math difficult to fathom, how about the aftermath? Who do you think will foot the bill for this misadventure? I will tell you. We are placing the bill squarely at the feet of our children and grandchildren, a debt sentence that will take many de-generations to repay.

Now of course, there are those in the Administration who insist we must fight fire with fire. Well, I've been talking with some firemen lately, and you know what? They say, "No Swami, actually you fight fire with . . . WATER." We should be dampening support for those terrorists, and instead we seem to be firing them up to spark off more incidents.

And this thing about pre-emptive war being a new policy —

not true. There's nothing new about it. It is old, very, very old, older than Machiavelli even. Now I know Mr. Bush sometimes gets his words mixed up, but Jesus did NOT say, "Doo doo unto others before they can doo doo unto you."

So if we need any more proof the Irony Curtain has descended, consider this: We have a Patriot Act that is unpatriotic, a President supported by the Christian Right perpetrating un-Christian wrongs, and a plan for peace that fans the flames of war. Can you say, "DUH? "

Disheartenment in the Heartland

No wonder there is disheartenment in the heartland. For with all the focus on the crisis in the Mid-East, we have failed to address the crisis in the Mid-West. For one thing, the average American is coming to realize our economy isn't shaping up because our jobs have shipped out. For another, people are slowly waking up to notice that the body politic is suffering from a severe case of parasites — a well-heeled predator class siphoning off our common wealth. Forget white-collar criminals. These are gold collar criminals.

Gold collar criminals are criminals who are big enough to actually help write the laws so that their crimes can become "lawful." Along with lots and lots of cash, another thing they have in their pockets are our legislative representatives. And it isn't just the Banana Republicans who are turning America into a banana republic. Parties in both parties have been partying on our dime, and the body politic is about ready to put its foot down and say, "Party's over!"

As if that isn't enough, the vicious dogma attack of 9/11 went right to the heart of America. And while we were recovering, we seemed willing to make the necessary lifestyle changes for a healthier heart: You know, reduce oil intake and go on a low-assault diet. But we just couldn't seem to stay away from the assault shaker, I guess, and we're guzzling more oil than ever. Add to this, the President's Big Iraq Attack and the ensuing Mad Cowboy Disease, and it's easy to see how the body politic has been put into a state of cattlepsy and herded into the bewilderness.

Sometimes Being Foolish Just Isn't Funny

And now there's more bad news. Apparently, the world is in such serious condition that the Earth's protective laugh force has been compromised. Scientists have discovered a hole in the Bozone Layer — our planetary clown chakra — because not enough levity is rising. Boy, talk about irony. You would think that with all this serious foolishness, more people would be laughing.

But sometimes being foolish just isn't funny, and we have to face the serious nature of our foolishness. And what foolishness it is! We have smart bombs, which is great. Now all we have to do is make sure our leaders are at least as smart as our bombs. And a smart leader? A smart leader knows when using even the smartest bomb is stupid.

Time to Wake Up Laughing

The good news is, we can break the chain of human foolishness by laughing lovingly at our human folly. When we wake up to the sound of our own laughter at our serious foolishness, it is called fool-realization. And it's even better when people from all sides are heartily laughing at the same thing. Imagine . . . side-splitting laughter coming from all sides can heal the split between the sides. Forget the sound of one hand clapping. For true spiritual perspective, nothing beats the sound of all sides laughing.

Now to rise to this level will require a lot of levity. That is why we need a Supreme Court Jester, so that we'll have someone to tell our leaders the truth, whether they want to hear it or not. And that is why each of us — no matter how serious things become — must allow ourselves to become an enlightening rod for bringing laughter to the political conversation, and helping others feel the levitational pull that counteracts all the gravity.

Take The Advice of a Political Guru and Check Into This Seven-Step Program

So what can be done? Can the body politic recover? Can we cure electile dysfunction? And who, pray tell, will bring all of this about? Now in the past, we've had the tendency to wish and pray for some Higher Force to intervene. Well now, I say it's time for us children of God to become adults of God as well — and take responsibility for our own planet. We cannot expect to be fed intervenously forever, you know.

As the "political guru," I will spell it out for you . . . G-U-R-U . . . gee, you are YOU! Listen, all you enlightened ones who are waiting for some kind of sign to get active — what are you waiting for? The world is going ape-shit, and you're blissfully waiting for the hundredth monkey? Time to go ahead and evolve, already. Time to wake up and say, "Well, I'll be a hundredth monkey's uncle, I AM the hundredth monkey!"

Talk about self-realization! Realizing each of us is a totally unique self in the body politic, and all of these healthy, active, activating selves standing firm — who needs Viagra? We can get a healthy election any time we want to!

That is why I have developed my Seven-Step Program, so that we the people can evolve into the conscious sovereign citizens our Founding Fathers dreamed of, and become truly worthy of the awesome legacy they've left us. Now, you might ask, why a Seven Step Program? Simple. It puts us five steps ahead of those twelve-step folks, and let's face it, time is of the essence!

So . . . are we ready to drive a new karma, and trade in that old Dodge for an Evolvo? Are we ready to face the music and dance together, and in the process teach the whole world some new steps to democracy? Are we ready to wake up laughing and leave laughter in our wake?

It has been said that each of us already has the answers within. Matching them with the corresponding questions, that is the challenge. So here are some questions to consider, some irony supplements to chew on, if you will, to begin a new conversation that will help build a strong body politic seven ways:

- What if we stopped pretending that what we don't know won't hurt us, and put an end to America's costly cruise down denial?
- What if we elected ourselves to make the world a happier place by improving reality?
- What if we let go of the idea that we're here to earn God's love, and embraced the notion that we are here to spend it?
- What if we tell a healing vision? We might even heal the television.

- What if we "voted" for these healing visions that improve reality with our attention, our time, and our money?
- What if we acted like fooly-realized sovereign citizens no longer afraid to laugh at own shadow?
- What if we stopped wasting precious energy and resources on getting even, and cultivated solutions so odd, that everyone wins?

So I say, everybody for precedent! As I toss my own turban into the ring and launch my world-win campaign for a new precedent, I ask all of you to climb on board and stand proudly on the Pro-Laugh platform. May we create a world where we use the light of loving laughter to illuminate darkness everywhere, especially in those poorly-lit corridors of power . . . a world where every born feed-us enjoys the right to life, and where we hear freedom ring in the sound of every child's laughter.

May we wake up laughing, and wake up loving. May God bless America, and God bless our precious, beautiful planet.

—Swami Beyondananda,
April 1, 2004

Let's Elect Ourselves!

Time to Act Like Citizens, Not Subjects

*"Government of the people, by the people,
for the people . . . people — **hey, that's us!"**

G reat news! We don't need a revolution in America. We already had one, thank you. Those very enlightened documents, the Declaration of Independence and the Bill of Rights, safeguard our right to freely exercise our will — or, our won't — in any way that makes us happy yet tramples no one else's freedom.

How the Body Politic Became a Couch Potato

Unfortunately, while we the people were busy doing other things like tending to our families and our gardens and making a living, we began to neglect our body politic. And you know what happens when you don't exercise your rights. The body politic becomes a 90-pound weakling, a pushover for anyone with a pushy agenda who just happens to have tons of money, a monopoly over the media, and plenty of followers to follow in lockstep. And before you know it, what once were citizens have become subjects.

Why Our Skeptic System Isn't Working

Meanwhile, the Irony Curtain has descended, as Americans have become walled off from the information they need to make wiser political choices. Instead, the mass media has inundated the body politic with so much toxic B.S., that our skeptic system has overflowed, and people end up swallowing huge ironies whole. How else would people allow the most unconstitutional and un-American document ever conceived to be called the "Patriot Act"? How else would people accept that the best way to protect our liberties is to . . . take them away?

A Cure for Impotence?

In 2002, those seeking an alternative looked to the Democratic Party, but alas. Ever since that electile dysfunction they suffered in Florida, those Democrats just can't seem to get an election, can they? But their impotence doesn't have to be our impotence. And if we the people revitalize not just the Democratic Party, but all parties in the body politic, the current regime will have stiff opposition in 2004.

Time for an American Evolution

The job of running the country is too big for one person, and even too big for a small, secretive cadre. So I say, *we* are elected. Lincoln spoke of government of the people, by the people and for the people. People — hey, that's us!

More than two centuries ago, our Founding Fathers put forth an unprecedented, revolutionary notion: Each of us is endowed by our Creator with inalienable rights . . . that we are essentially sovereign citizens choosing to align in government for our collective good. In other words, the government is meant to do our bidding, not the bidding of the highest bidder. So now, we the people must elect ourselves to become the empowered, enlightened citizens our Founding Fathers intended. Why now? Because it is too late to do it sooner!

=========== A Note from Swami ===========

In this topsy-turvy political environment ruled by impropaganda, sometimes something sounds truly plausible . . . and is simply not true. On the other hand, sometimes there are facts that are true, but are . . . Truly Unbelievable.

★ TRULY UNBELIEVABLE

Welcome to America, Where Nonvoters Rule, And Nobody Was Elected President!

As Will Rogers once said, "Figures don't lie, but liars figure." And judging by the figures below, the current batch of liars figure that more than half of the eligible voters in America are not likely to vote. Why not? Well, as another homespun wise guy, Jim Hightower, once noted, "If God had meant us to vote, He would have given us candidates." Apparently, voters in other democracies have candidates, because here are the statistics since 1991:

Australia	83%
Austria	78%
Belgium	84%
Canada	60%
Denmark	83%
Finland	71%
France	61%
Germany	72%
Greece	85%
Ireland	71%
Italy	90%
Luxembourg	60%
Netherlands	75%
Norway	76%
Portugal	79%
Spain	79%
Sweden	84%
Switzerland	38%
UK	72%
US	**45%**

The only country with lower turnout than the U.S. is Switzerland, and they don't need to vote because they have all the banks.

Here it is in black and white, folks. Nobody should be President. Nobody got more votes than Gore, Bush, Nader and anybody else combined, so Nobody won. Nobody was the people's choice. Which explains our poor voter turn-out. After all, what more efficient way to vote for Nobody than to not even show up?

Why Can't the Body Politic Sustain an Election?

It's puzzling, all right. We've been well-endowed by our Creator, we've inherited good, healthy freedom-loving genes from our Founding Fathers, so why shouldn't we be able to enjoy a healthy election? Well for one thing, the body politic has had to swallow so much toxic B.S. over the years, that we have a severe case of truth decay . . . those truths our Founding Fathers held self-evident have decayed into a cluster of petty self-interests, and the silenced majority is being out-shouted and out-spent by the noisy minority.

Political scientists tell us that one of the key causes of electile dysfunction is insecurity, and look at us. Ever since 9/11, the Administration has been selling insecurities like there's no tomorrow — telling us there might not be a tomorrow if we don't buy *their* security plan. The more insecure they make us feel, however, the more willing the body politic becomes to buy into an insecurity system that will only secure the security of our current

Administration. Like the little boy who cried Wolfowitz, our President keeps repeating the Neocon litany that the only way we can be safe is to attack first. But neo or retro, a con is still a con. Lies get repeated until they start to sound true and before we know it, bingo . . . we've got a serious case of truth decay.

Meanwhile, our skeptic system has become overloaded thanks to a constant onslaught of questionable information that is largely going unquestioned. Instead of providing the nutrition a body politic needs for strength and mental acuity, the impropaganda machinery offers us misinformation, disinformation, lots of dissing information to make sure we don't notice the *missing* information. And when the skeptic system isn't doing its job, the body politic responds by believing anything — or believing nothing. Either way, the result is impotence.

Do the Ends Justify the Meanness?

Meanwhile, the attack dogmas of the right wing have esteemrolled the opposition. Can I be blunt? Over the past ten years, the Republicans have been playing hardball. The Democrats have been playing hardly-have-balls. Assaholism has run rampant, and the current Administration's agenda is beginning to look a lot like "the final solution to the Democrat problem."

Now we all know the Presidency has always provided a bully pulpit, but that doesn't mean it has to come with a ready-made bully. Sadly, the combination of ignorance and arrogance, unparalleled in American history, has left our friends around the world mystified and mortified. And it's actually led to the coining of a new word — *ignoranus*.

In that sense, our President is indeed the Great Uniter. In less than four years in office, he has accomplished what no one has done since F.D.R. He has actually brought the Democrats together. Even more astounding than that, he has accomplished what experts have deemed impossible. He has so united the Iraqis that the Shiites have crossed over to the Sunni side of the street.

Thanks to President Bush, America is so unpopular that we actually nudged ahead of Al Qaeda for number one on the Worldwide Unpop Charts. How did we manage to do that in less than three years? The majority of the world's people now consider

5

our country more dangerous than religious fanatic suicide terrorists who blow up civilians. How could they believe such a thing? Maybe they don't get Fox News.

Meanwhile, back here behind the Irony Curtain, far too many Americans still believe that the ends justify the meanness. Truly we are caught between Iraq and a hard place. It's easy to justify going to war against a bunch of suicide murderers who believe they will get to heaven by putting everyone else through hell. It's harder to face how we have put so many innocent civilians through hell just to fuel our own little corner of relative heaven. When we are brave enough to peek behind the Irony Curtain, and look ourselves in the heart, we know that this escalating meanness can come to no good end.

Celebrate Man Hog Day — This November 2nd

There's a bumper sticker that says it all about electile dysfunction: "Democracy: Use it Or Lose It." Let's declare the first Tuesday in November, formerly called Election Day, "Man Hog Day." One day a year, the body politic needs to take emerge 'n see measures.

We need to emerge from our self-serving myths, and see our own shadow — otherwise we face four more years of darkness. For, unless we acknowledge and face our shadow, we will be endarkened by it. And while we're at it, this Man Hog Day let's ferret out some of those manhogs. The manhog is a modern mythical creature, half man, half hog. The current bunch of pigs at the trough are living high on the hog thanks to pork-barrel legislation. Time for we the people to bring home the bacon and say, "Th-th-th-th-that's all, folks!"

We Are the Precedent We've Been Seeking

We in this country are fortunate to have three branches of government, but what really keeps our tree of political life strong and healthy are not the branches, but the roots . . . and WE the people are the roots. If we want democracy to truly take root, it's time for upstanding citizens to stand up and take a stand!

We must elect ourselves. Hey, George Bush did it. Why not us?

If we don't want to follow the misleader going the wrong way down the wrong street, we must become the leaders we've been sorely missing. We must elect ourselves to lead: We must elect to tell the truth, to take responsibility, to be present in the present, to participate . . . and we must elect to evolve. Because this is, after all, the American Evolution.

Elect to Tell the Truth

It has been said that the truth will set you free — but first it will piss you off! You know how those 12-step programs always begin by acknowledging that we cannot make a change without the help of a Higher Power? Well, if we take a close and careful look at how government of the people by the people and for the people has devolved since the American Revolution, an appropriate response is, "God help us!"

Look at how far we've come in 225 years. We've gone from rising up against taxation without representation to lying down in the face of representation without taxation. Because it isn't just our jobs being out-sourced, it's our representation. Since we now can brag that we have the best government money can buy, the money that is buying our government quite often is based in a safe tax shelter offshore. Now I will say this about the current administration. They've made great strides in the area of minority representation. Never before in the history of our country has a President truly represented a smaller minority.

And our government's lack of credibility — it's incredible! Bill Clinton — remember him — he took an "out-turn" with an intern and his little peccadillo got blown all out of proportion. Meanwhile, George Bush was snuggled up in bed with that Lay from Enron who screwed millions. So here's a question: Why the big deal over Little Bill, and the little deal over the BIG bill the little people are being billed?

Just another news story that went under-covered while the media assaulted us with weapons of mass distraction. Like what happened at the 2004 Super Bowl. CBS — an aptly-named network which apparently only wants us to see the B.S. *they* want us to see — refused to run a MoveOn ad critical of George Bush. Meanwhile, their affiliate MTV (or *Empty Vee,* as it has come to be known), created a massive distraction by making sure we kept abreast of Janet Jackson. This is all too typical of mass media nowadays — an over-willingness to expose a little boob, and an under-willingness to expose a big one.

You know, I hate to say this about the world's biggest baddest superpower, but we are afraid of our own shadow. Otherwise, we would have the political will to uncover the cover-ups that have caused such disheartenment in the heartland. We the people — the true patriots who see that there can be no peace without justice, and no democracy without truth — we have to rise up and say, "We've been sold a bill of bads, and we're not buying it." Or, as the body politic was heard to utter right before it went unconscious, "My God, I've been bullshot!"

Elect to Take Responsibility

We Americans are the most litigious people in the history of the world. Although we make up less than 5% of the world's population, we are home to 50% of the world's lawyers. No wonder devout FUNdamentalists (accent on "fun") are praying for Nonjudgment Day when all our trials will be over, and hence all the lawyers will disappear. No wonder assaholism is so prevalent in our culture. Boy, talk about polluting the body politic. All that residoodoo from those lawsuits — political scientists call it "sue-widge" — has clogged our skeptic system, crippled enterprise, and made us as a people more defensive — and for that matter, more offensive too.

And it's not just lawyers. Everybody wants to get into the act. Like those people who are suing fast food companies for making them fat. No one yet has tried to sue a fork or spoon manufacturer for making instruments of mass-consumption, but someone probably will. If we freedom-loving people argue that there is indeed free will, well then there has to also be "free won't." Or maybe people in this country have been force-fed so much impropaganda that they actually go unconscious when they eat. That would explain why we, 4.5% of the world's population, consume 30% of the world's resources. With consumption being our consuming passion, it's no wonder so many of us are getting "super-sized."

Meanwhile, for the past few years our foreign policy has reinforced our image as a heavy. As a super-sized superpower, we've been casting a pretty large shadow. Maybe when we take responsibility and see our shadow, then respond responsibly we can begin to use our super powers more wisely. Just as we need to take responsibility for our own Big Mac attacks, we must also take responsibility for our government's Big Iraq attack to make sure we can sustain our oil-rich diet.

Time to step out of the shadows of casting responsibility elsewhere and face the truth: If we are citizens and not subjects, then our government is our responsibility. Just as we can voluntarily choose to not swallow unhealthy, fattening food, we can be responsible for not swallowing toxic, fear-mongering impropaganda. Elect yourself to tell the truth. Truth is like a weed. It cannot be contained for long, and it will pop up everywhere. Now you may have noticed that the current administration has been

9

doing everything in its power — and a lot of things not consti-tutionally in its power — to kill the weeds of truth before they sprout. So I say if enough of us tell the truth at the same time, they won't be able to use Round Up.

Elect to Be Present in the Present – and Participate

You know what the most popular metaphysical book was last year? "The Power of Now." That's right. I predicted that "The Power of Now" would be the next big thing, and it was. And now I have another prediction. Living in the now is the wave of the future, and time itself will become a thing of the past.

I remember many years ago when I was studying with the Garment Center Saint, Harry Cohen Baba, it occurred to me that so much of what we see on the news is not really that new. We've been doing the same old things for so long, no wonder so much of our news is old news. Maybe it should be called the "olds". I mentioned this to Harry Cohen Baba, and he said, "You don't like the old news? So *nu?* Make some new news."

And what better time to make new news than in a moment that's not yet happened? Since this particular "now" has never happened before, it's the perfect time to try something we've never done before. And who knows? We might have some new news on our hands.

Those who want to evolve into the enlightened citizens our Founding Fathers imagined need to recognize that indeed we are driving our own karma. If we are stepping away from the past, we no longer can afford to listen to those political and religious lead-ers who say, "Leave the driving to us." Let's stop avoiding respon-sibility, or in terms of karma, it's time to trade in that old Dodge for an Evolvo. And needless to say, let's relegate that Imperial to the antique karma museum. A big fat Imperial will only get you so far when the planet has run out of gas.

Elect to Evolve

This is the American Evolution, and that means each of us can choose to evolve. Now is the time to stop aping the worst human traits, and ascend to our higher destiny. This year — 2004 — is the

Chinese Year of the Monkey, a time when wild, creative ideas can be successful. Let's make it the Year of the Hundredth Monkey, when an uncritical mass of us humans evolve enough to achieve Nonjudgment Day. And when we release the monkey mind and embrace the human heart, all the fear-based impropaganda will fall on deaf ears, and they won't be able to monkey with our minds anymore.

We've all learned about its great stars, but the American Revolution included many stripes as well. Alexander Hamilton was an elitist who believed the people could not be trusted. Thomas Jefferson was a freethinker who believed the people had to be trusted. But they and others created the Constitution, the exquisite balance of powers that now is teetering on the edge of the teeter-totter.

At this time, the American Evolution must bring together wise people and constructive ideas from all shades of the political spectrum. We need to be conservative in using our precious resources, liberal in love and in service, and radical in imagination. And we need to do an end-run around the existing political parties, and bring the forces of Evolution front and center.

I recommend establishing the Front and Center Party, offering leading edge wisdom from the Radical Center. Calling all karmas, calling all karmas! All those who are ready to evolve from the realm of hierarchies and lowerarchies, from the world of domination and fear, time to come front and center. Time to live from those radically crazy ideas like the Golden Rule, instead of caving to "the Gold rules." Time to vote for the rule of law, not the rule of lawyers. Time to take a stand for those things all decent Americans stand for: Honesty, integrity, justice and kindness. After all, what use is a platform if no one stands on it? So speak with your feet and step up!

★ PROFILES IN ENCOURAGEMENT

The Day the World Stood Up

*I*n March of 2003, as American troops were dispatched to march into Iraq, a truly unprecedented event occurred. For the first time ever, a worldwide peace movement massed and marched for peace to show its support for non-lethal ways of dealing with the Iraq situation. After all, if the Iraqi people were truly being held hostage and Saddamized by a brutal dictator, what kind of hostage-saving program is it to go in and kill thousands of these poor hostages?

And in this amassing of the masses, a strong vital worldwide body politic started flexing its young muscles. To quote former UN Secretary General Robert Muller, "Now there are two superpowers. The U.S., and the merging voices of the people of the world." And those of us who are open to the radically odd idea that war might not be the best way to handle human conflict, we are part of that counter-balancing superpower. Time to embrace our superpowers, use our x-ray vision to see through the lies, and see that it's *right* that makes *might*, not the other way around.

SWAMI'S "TELL-A-VISION":
THE AMERICAN EVOLUTION HAS BEGUN

I have a dream. All over America, cells in the body politic are awakening, even those who slept through the last alarm. They are marching, joyfully declaring their independence, interdependence and innerdependence. The American Evolution has begun.

I see millions of self-elected citizens going on a fair and balanced Fox hunt, finally cornering the slippery, sly critter, shining the light of truth, and exposing weapons of mass deception.

I see the Boston TV Party, where millions toss their televisions and choose to tell a healing vision instead. After all, who needs mass media when the masses *are* the media?

One by one, I see hordes of American Evolutionaries taking up arms — and hugging a Republican. Or a Democrat. Or a Green, or a Libertarian . . . just as long as you're hugging a party from some other party. How else will we become a one party system, where it's one big party, and *everyone* is invited?

On November 2nd, I see millions of Evolvos cruising to the polling places, and I see the headlines on November 3rd:

"The American Evolution Has Begun . . .
The First Big Shot Has Been Fired!"

Now we all know which Big Shot needs to be fired first. But that is just the beginning. I see an evolutionary wave activating the body politic, until we've fired every other big shot who thinks that he or she is such a big shot, that they're above the law.

To Take America Forward,
We Must Take America Back . . . and Vice Versa

Howard Dean & Co. told us we must "take America back," and that's true. But if we really want to take America back, we must take America forward . . . into a new millennium that's really new, where we actually try new things with the intention of getting new results. And it is equally true that to take America forward, we must first take America back . . . and Vice Versa.

And this forward and back is a two-step, a de-Texas two-step if you will.

Step one is regime change.

Step two is revitalizing, re-energizing and de-Texing the body politic so that we never again slip into cattlepsy.

13

Now there are those who say there is virtually no difference between Kerry and Bush. If you believe that, you probably also believe there is no difference between verbal sexual harassment and rape.

There is a huge elephant standing on our neck, choking off the air passages for the body politic. Government of the people, by the people, for the people has not yet perished from the earth. But it is on life support. First, let's get the beast off of our neck. Then let's take that other party — the braying donkey — and turn it into a workhorse pack animal that supports true justice and the rights of people. And don't expect that stubborn beast to move itself. So, American Evolutionaries, I say . . . time to haul ass! Because we're in for the long haul, not just the short overhaul.

The American Evolution happens as each individual self in the body politic elects to elect themselves one by one. All of these strong, independent little elections standing side by side, I tell you, it's like Viagra for the body politic. And now that the body politic is getting some backbone — not to mention frontbone — the heart too must evolve. The body politic has been disheartened because the spirit politic has been dispirited — and now must be re-inspired.

We DO need a Higher Power, and the power of loving goodness is good enough for me. Very few people can say they've seen the face of God face to face, but each and every one of us has seen goodness, and goodness knows, we know what goodness feels like. Goodness feels good. I believe in Good. So how about this as the motto for the American Evolution: "One Nation, Under Good."

And we need other people. What good is good if there are no good people to share it with? As we Right-to-Laugh FUNdamentalists like to say, "All for fun . . . and fun for all!"

So let us renew our vows to be true to our freedom, our community, and the power of love we feel inside us and express outside us. It's time to re-declare our Independence. . . . our Interdependence. . . . and our Innerdependence . . .

. . . and may it all happen before we're all in Depends!

SWAMI ANSWERS YOUR QUESTIONS . . . AND YOU WILL QUESTION HIS ANSWERS.

A Few People Who Control Everything? What GREAT News!

Dear Swami:

The more I read, the more I see that there's really just a small group of individuals who have the power and influence to control just about everything on this planet. Am I missing something, Swami? Do I seem paranoid? And if this is true, is there any way to turn this negative into a positive?

—Ann M. Feddiman,
Scarsdale, New York

Dear Ann:

Well, first of all let me say that under the right conditions, paranoia isn't that bad a thing. I know a guy who has two afflictions: he is both paranoid and dyslexic. But he's been able to turn these two negatives into a positive. He is convinced that the world is plotting to make him happy, and there isn't a thing he can do about it.

But back to your first question. The notion that there is a just a handful of individuals pulling the strings is very, very good news. Why? Because it means there are a whole lot more of us than there are of them. I am reminded of a Zen Cohen my guru Harry Cohen Baba used to tell whenever any of his students felt disheartened by the power of a few. The Lone Ranger and Tonto found themselves trapped in a canyon in an ambush. The Lone Ranger turned to his companion and said, "Well, Tonto, we're surrounded by Indians. Looks like we're done for."

And Tonto said, "What you mean WE, kemosabe?"

The powers that be in power have been using weapons of mass distraction for years to weaken the body politic. By magnifying the issues that separate us, by making sure each side is fully enlisted in the culture wars, they are able to steal our money and our power while we're busy being outraged by Janet Jackson's boob or Mel Gibson's passion. The good news is, the body politic is awakening from a deep slumber and honest people from the left and from the right are beginning to shout encouragement to each other from across the chasm.

Although the last thing a two-party system needs is a fifth party, I'm calling for a new party, The Front and Center Party. All those who seek a government that does our bidding, not the bidding of the highest bidder, that provides transparency rather than the apparent trance we have now, time to come Front and Center. I invite these people to do an end run around the two polarizing parties and meet in the middle, and say, "Forget us vs. them. When it comes to wanting liberty and justice — we're all US!"

A Channeled Message From the Fifth Dimension

Dear Swami:

For years, we've been hearing about this Age of Aquarius they talk about, but look what we've got — perpetual warfare, the makings of a police state, economic and environmental degradation. Where's the harmony and understanding? Where's the sympathy and trust? Are we dealing with dyslexic astrology, or is this a cruel joke? When can we expect this Age of Aquarius, anyway?

—Dewey Matter,
Sebastopol, California

Dear Dewey:

Yes, this is a Frequently Asked Question, all right. Everywhere I go in this country, people are saying, "I could have sworn I voted for 'West Wing'? How'd we end up with the 'Sopranos'?"

Well, the good news is, the Age of Aquarius is indeed on its way — but first we must go through the Age of Nefarious — because, hey, doesn't any good quest involve a test? And we can shorten the time frame of the Nefarian Age with our conscious, loving, laughing actions. How do I know? Well, I posed the very same question in a recent meditation, and the answer I got can only be described as a channeled message from the Fifth Dimension:

When the goon moves into Lincoln's House
And stupider aligns with Mars
Then greed will rule the planet
And fear, obscure the stars
This is a warning, it's the Age of Nefarious
The Age of Nefarious . . . Nefarious . . . Nefarious

Harmony and understanding
Sympathy and trust don't count here
Just a twisted cynic mission
Breeding fearfulness, division
Time to tell a brand new vision
Go for fusion 'stead of fission
Turn Nefarious . . . to Aquarius
Nefarious to Aquarius
No nefarious . . . go Aquarius!

Let the sun shine
Let the sun shine in
The sun shine in
Let the sun shine (solar power)
Let the sun shine in (transparency in government!)
Let the Son shine (the Divine light of Soul power)

The Son shine in (the real heart of Jesus — it's do unto others,
    George, not doodoo)
Let it shine . . .

Nader Ran, Bush Won — and We Got Lots of Gore

Dear Swami:

I've always been a big admirer of Ralph Nader. He's been a great consumer advocate for the past forty years, and an individual of highest integrity. His policies for America would turn this country around, and under most circumstances, he'd have my vote. But this year, I'm not sure. Swami, how do you feel about Ralph Nader running?

—Doris Y. Dopen,
Decatur, Georgia

Dear Doris,

I would LOVE to see Ralph Nader run. In fact, I volunteer to lead the mob that chases him. You know, back in 2000 Nader said there was very little difference between Bush and Gore, and he was right — sort of. We ended up with Bush — and we got plenty of gore. Ralph Nader, of all people, should see that the current administration is unsafe at any speed. I agree with Ralph that we need to change direction — but first, we must apply the brakes and stop this idiot driver taking this country full speed ahead the wrong way down the wrong road.

Regime Change = Routine Change

Dear Swami:

I notice you're more than willing to make jokes about George Bush and the Republicans, and yet I haven't seen you poking fun at the Democrats and liberals. Why don't you go after some of the things they've done?

—Newcombe Gladley,
Arlington, Virginia

Dear Newcombe:

How can I make fun of what the Democrats have done when they've hardly done anything recently? As far as I can tell, they're still running on the fumes from the New Deal. But I hear your concern, so let me set the record straight: Each night before retiring, I fervently pray to have a Democrat in the White House to joke about. Truly, I look forward to doing jokes about how we're spending too much money on health, education, and preserving the environment. I look forward to having the whole world laughing with us, instead of at us. Frankly, I'm tired of making fun of the Banana Republicans, and like many Americans I'm coming to feel that George Bush simply isn't funny anymore. So, please . . . help out this poor cosmic comic. Vote for regime change this year, so I can have "routine change" next year.

How to Vote Every Day

Dear Swami:

I'm one of those people who hasn't voted in years. Maybe it's just being busy and overwhelmed with so many details in my own life and my family's life, maybe it was just being turned off to all the lies and rhetoric, but I guess I just went unconscious. Now, I'm awake. I'm motivated. I'm ready to vote. Only now, we have the Diebold voting machines — very easy to hack and manipulate — and I fear my vote won't count. What's an awakened citizen to do?

—Jim Schortz,
Waukegan, Illinois

Dear Jim:

I can completely understand your being numbed by the onslaught of media B.S., and it is good to see so many people awakening from the coma. Skeptics and cynics have been predicting the demise of our democracy for 200 years now, and it's almost a cliché that in each generation, we must stand up and protect our freedom. Usually this means standing on foreign soil with a weapon. For this generation it means standing on our own soil, unarmed except for the Declaration of Independence and the Constitution. If we want to avoid democracy dying at the hands of a Diebold, we must choose to live bold. Here are three ways we can elect ourselves to make sure our vote counts:

√ **Tell-A-Person.** In this electronic age, an ancient form of communication has been rediscovered — tell-a-person! Here is how it works: In the walk and talk of daily life, let people know that there is evidence that some party hacks have been hacking our voting machines. In fact, I say sandwich boards are coming back into style, but a button would work just as well: "I Lost 30 Rights in 30 Months. Ask Me How!"

√ **Celebrate Columbo's Day.** How about a new holiday named after the great TV detective, where we the people emulate Columbo and ask unasked questions and question unquestioned answers: "Now let me get this straight. There's no paper trail to these voting machines, they can be easily hacked by the folks who manufacture them, and the companies that manufacture them are all large contributors to the Republican Party. Oh, and some of the company executives have been convicted of fraud and embezzlement. No, no . . . nothing wrong. I'm just thinking out loud."

√ **Call in the UN, and have mandatory exit polling.** It couldn't be more convenient. The UN is headquartered right here in the United States, so it shouldn't be too expensive to have overseers from overseas oversee our elections. Meanwhile, if each of the 50 million + people ready for the American Evolution were to contribute just a dollar, this would pay for any major polling company to reinstitute the exit polls. Anything more than a 5% discrepancy would be cause for a recount. Exit polls would be worthwhile just to make sure that democracy itself isn't ushered out the exit.

But Seriously, Folks . . .

Are you in favor of perpetual warfare, growing gap between rich and poor, environmental destruction, loss of civil liberties?

Are you in favor of gold collar criminals buying influence in our government and siphoning off our national wealth?

You're not? Well then, the very least you can do is register to vote — and then vote! Expecting regime change without voting is like expecting to win the lottery without buying a ticket.

Remember to vote every day in every way with your dollars, your attention, your intention and your time.

Improve Reality!

From Original Sin to Humanifest Destiny

*"Why don't we go for heaven on Earth
— just for the hell of it?"*

In the aftermath of the 9/11 attack, a high-ranking military official inadvertently told the truth when he blamed the attack on "a failure of human intelligence." Truer words have rarely been spoken. With all of the spiritual wisdom and technical know-how available to us to create peace and plenty on this planet, why do we spend so much of our precious livelihood on weapons of deadlihood? No wonder the 'hood is so deadly. Not much applied human intelligence there!

Which Wolf Are We Feeding?

I have good news. There will indeed be peace on earth. Whether we humans are around to enjoy it is up to us. Because we have free choice. There is the story of the Native American grandfather who tells his grandson about two wolves fighting inside of him. One is the wolf of love and peace, the other the wolf of fear and warfare. "Which wolf will win, grandfather?" asks the boy.

"Whichever one I feed," the grandfather replies.

Humanifest Destiny

Right now, we have two dueling dualities offering opposing worldviews: Original Sin vs. Humanifest Destiny. There are those who insist that humans are natural born losers who can only be saved by the Grace of God. Others who believe in the human potential movement insist that despite all the contrary evidence, we do indeed have the potential to be human. Since I myself am a happy medium, I come down squarely in the middle. I believe in creationism and in evolution, that God created us humans with the ability to evolve in consciousness. Otherwise, Jesus would have said, "Now don't do a thing till I return." Instead, he (and all of the other great spiritual teachers) instructed us to "Love Thy Neighbor" and live by the Golden Rule.

Thrival, Not Survival

So we get to choose which reality we feed. We can live our love, or live our fear. We can play what R. Buckminster Fuller called the World Game — using our resources and imagination to create a world that works for everyone — or continue down the familiar path of "I win/you lose" and end up playing the End-of-the-World-Game. Survival? Been there, done that. Our spiritual teachings — not to mention common sense — tell us that we humans are destined for something better — thrival.

E Pluribus Unum

Time to get our World Game faces on, folks. Time to apply ourselves to a goal bigger than us, and choose a game worthy of REAL human intelligence. America has a powerful motto: E Pluribus Unum — out of many, One. The complete thrival of all the individual cells of the body politic making one healthy whole. Free individuals pursuing their happiness while using the Golden Rule as an operating principle to improve reality. Who needs a bailout from above? This is do-it-yourself home planet improvement — supply-side spirituality!

★ TRULY UNBELIEVABLE

War Beats Peace 397 Billion to Nothing!

Dollars Spent, 2003
On Military

Dollars Spent, 2003
Establishing a Department
of Peace

$397 billion

$ 0

397,000,000,000 to nothing. Well, now we know the score. But wait, there's more:

√ $397 billion is more than our government spends on education, transportation, healthcare, housing, and commerce combined.

√ The 2003 U.S. military budget exceeds the budgets of the next 25 nations combined and accounts for more than 36% of total world military spending.

√ Just $13 billion — about 3% of what we spend on our military each year — would feed and provide basic healthcare for all of the world's poor for a year.

√ $19.5 billion — about 5% of our yearly military budget — would provide healthcare for all of the uninsured children in the United States.

One B2, or To Be One?

Now it goes without saying a government must defend its people, and at the same time it's up to the people to defend themselves against an overly-defensive government using "defense" as a defense. Any time our fearless leaders don't want to tell us something, they throw it behind defense. If we really want to improve reality, we must elect ourselves to say, "Excuse, me. Can I see what you're hiding behind defense?" Who knows how much spare change we might find that could be used for something other than destruction.

Here's an example. The B2 bomber. Now the B2, in case you didn't know, was built in secret. Imagine how shocked Congress was in 1988 to find that we'd already spent $22 billion on something they didn't even know they had: A bomber designed to drop a nuclear payload on the Soviet Union, just in time for the fall of the Berlin Wall. Oh well. We could still use it, maybe.

The B2 was retrofit it for good old conventional weapons, and it finally had a shot at the majors in 1999 when it was used to bomb Kosovo. We still have a bunch of them, each of which cost $2.2 billion to build. Now . . . follow my logic here . . . what if we made the world a little bit safer (not a whole lot safer, just a little bit safer) so we could do without building just one teeny-weeny bomber like this? What if we took the $2 billion we spend on each B2 bomber, and used it to create something that benefits all? We could use one B2 . . . to be One. Maybe if we focused more of our resources on being One, we wouldn't need the B2.

Here are a few ways we could spend that $2 billion:

✓ We could give 200,000 teachers a $10,000 per year raise.

✓ We could buy 2 million underprivileged kids each a $1,000 computer.

✓ We could offer 20 million Bush voters a $100 gift certificate for a psychic reading at Seers so they could find out just what on earth they were thinking.

✓ We could give 200 million taxpayers a $10 refund — with the provision that they spend it in their own community. Money spent locally generates five times its value in goods and services!

"Please mom . . . Can't I have one?"

So there we have it. With just a slight shift in priorities, we can send a wave of healing energy rippling through the worldwide body politic. Shift happens, one way or another. Might as well make the shift into a higher and safer gear. And remember, when we make necessary changes in small increments, they're less likely to come in large excrements. Compare the results. One B2. Or, to be One. You decide.

One B2
- Top Secret . . . totally designed in secrecy.
- Designed to deliver nuclear payload.
- Fitted to launch conventional weapons.
- Puts fewer pilots in harm's way.

To Be One
- No secret at all . . .everyone knows there is a need for healing in the world.
- Designed to deliver new clear payload.
- Fit to launch unconventional weapons, such as love, goodness and kindness.
- Puts way, way fewer pilots in harm's way.

So What's In the Way, Anyway?

So what's with us? How come we don't spend more of our liveli-hood making the 'hood more lively? We should know by now that when the 'hood lacks livelihood, only the deadly hoods pre-vail, so of course the 'hood becomes more deadly. And then we're told that we have to defend ourselves because the 'hood is so dan-gerous, and the whole cycle of viciousness begins again.

Then there are those people who insist that we're just wasting our time thinking that things in the world could be better. Interestingly enough, these tend to be the people who are doing just fine with things the way they are. These shortsighted and wrong-headed beliefs then end up circulating through the body politic and weak-ening it, causing irony-deficient, anemic thoughts. Like, for example:

You can't fight city hall.
It's always been this way, and it's always gonna be this way.
Poverty, war, and starvation . . . they've always been with us,
    and they always will.
Of course it's corrupt. What do you expect?
It's a bad world out there. Good thing we have our government
    to protect us.

Conclusion? Reality can't be improved. Well, our Founding Fathers beg to differ. Those wild and crazy guys believed it was self-evident we were born into a world that we could co-create into a place with more freedom, more justice, more opportunity, where we could pursue happiness to our heart's content without the King's police pursuing us. If it's true reality can't be improved, we in this country might still believe:

You can't fight King George.
There's always been slavery, and there will always be slavery.
Ordinary people living past forty? Now who came up with that
    ridiculous idea?
Of course those Negro folks should sit at the back of the bus.
    It's the natural order of things.
It's a bad world out there. We should make sure our women are
    completely covered up, and we should kill them if they aren't.

Call me a hopeless hopium addict, but I hold to the optimystic view that we humans are trainable, and have in fact evolved out of much coarser behavior. Otherwise, if I told you, "We'd love to have you for dinner sometime," you wouldn't know whether to dress up or bring an apple for your mouth.

Now of course, there are still toxic conditions in the world — largely due

"Sit!...Stay!"

to toxic conditioning. Indeed, it's a mind field out there filled with toxic beliefs, and you have to watch very carefully where you step. Never mind looking out for number one. These days, you gotta look out for number two.

What People Believe – It's Unbelievable!

I had a dream there was an invention that completely changed the world, as we know it: A foolproof B.S. detector. I'm not sure exactly how it would work, but it might be like a remote that you aim at political leaders, and it filters out all of the lies. It would be like watching TV with the sound off, for the most part. A more sophisticated model might even have subtitles that run underneath the narrative and translate twisted spin into what is really being said.

No doubt about it, thanks to a massive media that never rests, the B.S. factories are running full throttle. Now there are some jobs that haven't been out-sourced. Artists starve in America, but not B.S. artists. Now we're all adults here, and we all know what B.S. stands for: Belief System. And like any other B.S., the most dangerous belief system is the one we don't realize is a belief system. Believing in a belief? No problem. But refusing to believe that our beliefs are just beliefs has caused unbelievable problems and suffering in the world.

Another useful caveat about belief . . . the word "believe" has a lie smack dab in the middle of it, sort of like the bull lurking behind every sacred cow. Nothing wrong with getting nourishment out of the sacred cow, by getting to the heart of the matter. But beware of the bull! As my guru Harry Cohen Baba used to say, "Truth resides in the heart. Belief lies in your head." So the best way to avoid the lies in your head is to focus on the love in your heart.

Here's another radical idea. What if we stopped believing so much in beliefs, and actually noticed what works? Now take the current Administration — please! Seeing is believing all right, and that's why they instruct their intelligence forces to show them only what they want to see. That way, they can continue believing whatever they want to believe, even when it completely defies intelligence.

In case you've been baffled as to the political choices people make in this country, baffle no more. Here is the truly unbelievable truth in an actual quote from a real human being. After being told of a particularly egregious perpetration (backed by ample evidence) by the powers that be in power, one individual actually said, "Well that may be true, but I don't believe it."

What Kind of Mystic Are You?

There are two kinds of people in this world: The kind of people who divide people into two kinds of people, and the kind who don't.

If you don't look kindly on those who believe there are two kinds of anything, then please don't read this section. But if you yourself are a mystic, or have had the urge to consult a mystic, it is useful to know that there are two kinds of mystics in the world — the optimystics, and the pessimystics. The pessimystics are very much in touch with reality. But the optimystics are happier and live longer for some reason. The pessimystics are the ones who are lamenting, "The sky is falling, the sky is falling!" The optimystics say, "No. It only looks that way because *we* are ascending."

So if it's all belief systems anyway, and we can choose what B.S. we believe, why not adopt a pet belief that will improve reality? There are belief systems that tend to hurt, and there are those that tend to heal. The beliefs we subscribe to determine how we see the world. So if you notice yourself subscribing to fearful limiting beliefs, cancel your subscription. And subscribe to something else. There are more helpful beliefs to have, like the belief in the loving heart of goodness.

And by the way, all of the great mystics tell us — when we look past the yimmer-yammer that others have used to twist their teachings into systems of control — that truth is truly beyond belief. It's like the time the renowned physicist Neils Bohr was being interviewed by a journalist, who was surprised to notice a horseshoe above the Nobel Laureate's office door. She said, "Dr. Bohr, you're a great scientist. Surely you don't believe that a horse shoe is going to bring you good luck."

"Of course not," he said. "I think it's nonsense."

"Well then," she persisted, "why is the horseshoe up there?"

"Oh," replied Dr. Bohr, "because it works whether you believe in it or not."

★ PROFILES IN ENCOURAGEMENT

The Bucky Stopped Here . . . And Started Over

In 1927, 32-year-old R. Buckminster Fuller was an abject failure. He had been bounced out of Harvard, failed at every business he tried, and now was on the verge of bankruptcy. He realized that his wife and young child would be financially better off with him out of the picture. He stood ready to end his life and hurl his miserable self into Lake Michigan, when suddenly a wild idea occurred to him. If he was going to throw his life away, why didn't he "donate his life to science" instead? Instead of wasting the gift of life, he would lead his life as "an experiment." He lived more than 50 more years, and became one of the world's most innovative thinkers, inventors and visionaries. He invented the geodesic dome, coined terms such as "spaceship earth," and influenced millions with his concept of the World Game — a world that works for everyone. And like the "perfect Ponzi scheme" where everyone wins, his life-affirming visions have radiated out and birthed untold projects and products that helped make the world a more functional and loving place. He crammed so much living into one lifetime that I've often said, "If we had more people like Bucky Fuller, we'd need fewer people!"

Drive Your Karma, Curb Your Dogma

As a happy medium, I am often asked, "What is the secret for happiness in this life?" And as a blabbermouth who just can't keep a secret, I always spill the beans: Unhappiness comes from the absence of happiness. To make sure you never run out, always take happiness with you. That way you'll always have it wherever you go.

But if you really want to have happiness for yourself — and have a surplus of it left over for others — my advice is simple: Drive your karma, and curb your dogma. Now it's true we human beings have had dogmas since the dawn of recorded history, and this is understandable. You cannot imagine how comforting it is to curl up with a warm, fuzzy dogma on a dark night of the soul. Some dogma-lovers keep them around for protection. It's reassuring to have a guard dogma to scare away frightening thoughts — and it's great to have a pet belief to fetch you an explanation after a hard day at the office. Indeed, dogma is mind's best friend.

But we have only to look at the events of 9/11 to see how devastating a vicious dogma attack can be. And that is why it is so important to preserve happiness in the world, to never unleash a mad dogma irresponsibly. Another fact of life is that dogmas eventually get sick and old, and may need to be put down. And sadly, there are those who spend so much time walking their dogma, that they never get their karma out of the garage.

In the old days we thought we were driven by our karma. But now, more and more people are coming to realize that we can drive our own karma. And where do we drive our karma? On the expressway, of course. Any way you choose to express your love, joy and talent in the world, that is your expressway. Just think. Every one of us selves in the vast body politic has been given a special gift, just for entering. So you are already a winner! What if we were here to use our gifts on behalf of wholeness? What if we were here to "be fruitful and multiply" and plant olive trees instead of land mines? What if we were here to squeeze the living heaven out of everything in this life? Hey, even if we just pretended that was the case, the world would be greatly improved!

Practice Fun Do, and Fung Shun

No doubt about it, people are busier nowadays. In fact, people are having so much difficulty cramming all their activities into a limited amount of time that I have heard reports that we are on a crash course to run out of time a lot sooner than we previously believed. If things get bad enough, we might actually have to go to an eight-day week. Imagine how much pressure it would release to have just one extra day a week. Me, I'd place that extra day right between Sunday and Monday and call it Funday.

"There was sand in it yesterday!"

All of this busyness as usual has created undue stress, and this undue stress due to all this doing . . . could very well be our undoing. Because let's face it, stress is stressful. I cannot stress enough how stressful stress can be. And so much of that stress is self-inflicted. Even though deep inside we know that we are always here and it is always now, it seems that all we're ever doing is trying to get somewhere else so we can be there then. And then, when we get there (wherever there is) we wish we were back here. And there you are.

Many in western society suffer from what humorologists call the Sinatra Syndrome . . . a "doo-be-doo-be-doo" imbalance that comes from too much doing, and not enough being. I have often said, if you're getting over-stressed being a doer, relax and do a beer instead. But for far too many, it's do, do, do, until one day they realize their whole life is doodoo.

Doing in balance is important, so we must ask ourselves two questions: Who am I being while I am doing the doing? And is what I am doing reflect the being I want to be? Clearly, we are here to do something, otherwise we'd just be watching life on TV. And why shouldn't that something we do be improving reality? There are two ancient daily practices I recommend to improve not just your own reality, but the reality of everyone around you: Fung Shun and Fun Doo.

The practice of Fung Shun is where the Spirit meets the road, where all the heavy-duty light workers come down from their lofty ideals to deal with the funky junk in the so-called "real world." Fung Shun is the application of the ideal to the real-deal on a daily basis. So here is the simplest formula for the daily practice of improving reality: Turn the funk into function, leave the junk at the junction.

Fun Doo is another radical concept, because it suggests that what we spend forty plus hours a week doing should not just improve reality but should also be fun. You may scoff, but Fun Doo sure beats all the unfun doodoo so many of us spend our time doing. I once asked my guru, Harry Cohen Baba, "How do we know when we are both happy and successful in life?"

He replied, "When you can unequivocally answer yes to the question, 'From THIS you make a LIVING?'"

Of course, we all know that life is not always fun. So what do we do then? Well. the next best thing is to have fun not having fun — creative complaining, this is called. But when you're not having fun, and not having fun not having fun, you can still MAKE fun of whatever it is that isn't fun.

Laughter Improves Reality!

Don't laugh — but laughter is one of the most potent medicines for improving reality instantly. We may not notice it because it isn't sold over the counter (although some drug stores are beginning to sell canned laughter, but by prescription only). But leading humorologists say that the amount of comedy found in the average one-liner (about one Youngman of laughter) can heal up to a megahurt of emotional pain! And this isn't surprising because when we let the bells of laughter ring, we are pealing away layers of fears and frustrations. No doubt about it, levity lightens us up and helps us lose weightiness.

And that is why we FUNdamentalists (accent on *fun*) have founded the Pro-Laugh movement, and the Right-to-Laugh Party. If we really want to improve reality, we must laugh in the face of ridiculous nonsense that is causing unnecessary suffering in the world. As more and more of us wake up laughing and leave laughter in our wake, healing farce fields are formed, and it raises the laugh force on the planet. It's an undeniable truth. Gravity makes us sad, while levity makes us happy. Increased happiness improves reality, and improved reality increases happiness. So, before going any further, I ask that you read the Right-To-Laugh Humanifesto, and take a vow of levity. The laugh you save may be your own.

The FUNdamentalist HUMANifesto Credo
of the The Right-To-Laugh Party
"One big party, everyone is invited . . . All for fun, and fun for all"

We believe that every born feed-us has the right to laugh, liberty, and the pursuit of happiness, unless of course happiness is a warm gun, in which case some restrictions may apply.

We have the right to laugh at our leaders, particularly those times when their actions are either seriously foolish or foolishly serious. We have the right to help them laugh with each other and at themselves, and if they're incapable of doing that, we have the right to laugh them out of power.

We have the right to laugh at the obscene foolishness of spending so much of our precious livelihood on weapons of deadlihood, and at the utter absurdity of doing the same things that haven't worked in the past — and expecting them to work in the future.

We propose creating the office of Supreme Court Jester to encourage citizens to use the light of laughter to illuminate the shadow, especially those poorly lit corridors of power.

We seek to extend this Right to Laugh all across the globe, especially places where things just aren't funny.

We propose that the United Nations and all levels of government begin each session with the Hokey Pokey. You put your whole self in . . . that is commitment. You pull your whole self out . . . that is detachment. You turn yourself around, and that is transformation . . . and that's what it's all about!

Join the Right-To-Laugh Party Now!

*W*e believe the problem is serious . . . but the solution is humorous. It's a scientific fact. The best way to overcome gravity is with levity. So all those who want to take a vow of levity . . . Please Rise!

Put your hand on your jocular vein and recite the Right to Laugh Pledge: "All for fun . . . and fun for all!"

Congratulations! You have now joined farces with the pro-laugh movement to raise the laugh-force and increase laugh-expectancy on this amazing planet.

May we all wake up laughing, and leave laughter in our wake. For truly the FARCE is with us.

OFFICIAL DISCLAIMER

NOTICE. Although we are enthusiastically pro-laugh, we are pro-choice as well. We respect each and every individual's right not to laugh. If you want to be miserable, go right ahead. Whatever makes you happy.

✪

SWAMI ANSWERS YOUR QUESTIONS . . . AND YOU WILL QUESTION HIS ANSWERS

Do We Deserve to Be Happy?

Dear Swami:

When I see how many humans behave, I have to question whether we humans are worthy of happiness in the first place. Don't you think it's a bit arrogant to think we actually deserve to have it any better than we do?

—Ronna DeMille,
Studio City, California

Dear Ronna:

Interestingly, I posed that very question to my guru, Harry Cohen Baba, and he told the following Zen Cohen: It was Yom Kippur, the Jewish Day of Atonement. The lawyer, the doctor and the banker were all in the front row of the synagogue. As was the custom, each was beating his breast and declaring his unworthiness: "I'm unworthy! I'm unworthy! I'm unworthy!" Just then, the lowly janitor walked in. Observing the scene, he too walked to the front and began crying out, "I'm unworthy! I'm unworthy! I'm unworthy!"

At which point, the lawyer turned to the banker and said, "So look who thinks he's unworthy!"

Ever since that great philosopher said, "I think, therefore I am," we've been giving the mind descartes blanche. So let's give the head a little rest, and relax in knowing that life is indeed a joke, but God is laughing with us not at us. The Creator is watching the Comedy Channel, and we are what's on. If God is laughing, who are we not to laugh? And if we are the Creator's primary source of entertainment and amusement, we should definitely cut ourselves a little slack.

Can Laughter Truly Heal?

Dear Swami:

I've been hearing for years that laughter can actually heal, but I wonder if you have any evidence. I'm skeptical.

—Juan Leiner
New York, New York

Dear Juan:

I'm surprised that you haven't heard about Norman Cousins. About thirty-five years ago, he was diagnosed with a life-threatening illness. Instead of checking into a hospital, he checked into a hotel room with Marx Brothers movies and "Candid Camera" reruns, and he got well. And when he cured himself, the medical establishment decided to study the healing power of humor. I guess the thinking was, well, it works in practice, but does it work in theory?

And they did discover that laughter produces endorphins, our body's natural painkillers. Laughter improves immune function. And laughter lowers blood pressure, because when we laugh it causes our blood vessels to dilate — which is better than having them die early.

If you need any further proof that laughter is good for you, there is the now-famous experiment where a group of college students were put in a room and given hilarious comedy videos to watch. Meanwhile, another group of students were put in another room. This group had to memorize Croatian parables, and they were given an electric shock each time they made a mistake. The results were conclusive. The group watching the comedy had more fun.

Does This Existence Really Exist?

Dear Swami:

Anyone who has studied any transcendent path knows that

"life is but a dream" and this physical plane is just an illusion. So why would anyone bother trying to change the world?

—Harry Krischner,
Ithaca, New York

Dear Harry:

I certainly agree with you that it is a waste of energy to try to change the world. I say, let's toilet train the world, and we'll never have to change it again. We have created one messy diaper, and even those who have ascended as high as you would have to agree, our human mess stinks to high heaven.

I also agree with you that this is all an illusion, but I tell you what. Somebody gives you a kick right in your illusions, it is still going to hurt. And yes, life is a dream. But because of toxic conditioning, for far too many, life is a bad dream. So here we are, dreamers in a dream, choosing what kind of dream we want to dream up. All those who want to dream a bad dream, raise your hands. I rest my case.

Yes Rev. Falwell, There Is Life After Birth

Dear Swami:

I don't understand how all of these "pro-life" people can be in favor of war. And why is there such an emphasis on war, anyway? There is the war on drugs, the war on poverty, the war on terrorism. Why war, Swami?

—Ella Mentry,
Clifton, Arkansas

Dear Ella:

Yes, the whole concept "pro-life" has puzzled me too. As soon as the unborn fetus becomes a "born feed-us," these people seem to lose interest. There needs to be some perspective here. I figure the entire time we spend in the womb — give or take a couple of weeks — is nine months. If we live to be 75 years old, that's 900 months. So it seems to me, to keep things balanced those "pro-life" people need to put a hundred times more attention on the "born" than the "unborn." This would greatly improve the reality the unborn get born into.

Regarding war, I'm afraid that our current leaders are fossils fueled by fossil fuels. And to the reptile mind, everything looks like war. Like the war on drugs. I've got a better idea that's simpler, cheaper and more effective: Forget the war on drugs — improve reality instead!

If we want to get away from the "war" mentality (and I have to say this is indeed a "men"-tality because more men than women buy into it), we must use our male energy to build bridges instead of blowing them up. The real pro-life movement is men and women who build the future and heal the past, laugh at the material in the material world, and use it as a true human growth hormone to grow into our full human potential.

But Seriously, Folks . . .

After all the philosophy, the religion, the soul-searching, does it really come down to "It's either you or me"? Is this what our spiritual teachings teach us? Is this the best we humans can do?

What if all the people in the world took a vote, and did what all the religions of the world — in principle — have been imploring us to do for millennia: No killing. No stealing. No false witness. What if we started with just these three, okay? We can see how we do with these, and if we feel the need to add on any more basic rules, fine. But right now, just these three.

How many people worldwide would vote to uphold and practice those three? How many would say, "No! We want to continue killing?" Good. That makes things a lot easier. Let's find these people, gather them on a remote island, and put US out of their misery.

Pray It Forward

And Practice Supply-Side Spirituality

"We're not here to earn God's love, we're here to spend it."

We believe in supply-side spirituality, so here is the spiritual bottom line: We are either feeding the wolf of love, or the wolf of fear. Good news. The human impulse toward love is stronger than it is to fear. Otherwise, these songs might have made the Top 40:

All You Need is Fear
Fear Is a Many-Splendored Thing
She Fears You, Yeah Yeah Yeah

Life Is FUNdamentally Fun

Yes, the lines have been drawn between FUNdamentalism (accent on fun) and fundaMENTALism (accent on mental). Do we extend the Right to Laugh to everyone and pray for the happiness of all beings, or do we insist that only we are going to heaven, and everyone else can go to hell?

FundaMENTALism
- Heaven is above us.
- Our way is the One Way.
- Frown upon laughing.
- Armageddon & Judgment Day.
- They stone you.

FUNdamentalism
- Heaven is where we make it.
- One way? Do not enter.
- Laugh upon frowning.
- Disarmageddon & Nonjudgment Day.
- They get stoned on their own.

Yes, You CAN Teach An Old Dogma New Tricks

Now the good news is, you can indeed teach an old dogma new tricks. In fact, you can even teach your dogma to heal! Each and every religion, no matter how dark its history, can be part of the Pluribus that adds up to Unum. My guru, Harry Cohen Baba, "the Garment Center Saint," was Jewish, had a Hindu ashram, and prayed to Buddha and Jesus. He explained, "Listen, any of these could be right. So why put all your begs in one askit?"

"Blisskrieg" Declared: All Out Peace!

Here is more good news: God is bigger than religion. So, even when religion doesn't work, prayer still does. You know the old saying, "Why throw the Baby Jesus out with the bathwater?" That is why we have launched a blisskrieg and declared "all out peace." Yes, all of the inner peace we have been cultivating all these years, time to let it all out. This is the piecemeal approach to peace. A little peace here, a little peace there, and pretty soon you've got one big peace everywhere.

How to Create Disarmageddon Instead of Armageddon

Imagine, as Bucky Fuller maintained, that we are all passengers and crew on Spaceship Earth. Wouldn't it make sense for all of us to pray for the success of our Mission? That is what the blisskrieg is, sending waves of love and light to elevate everyone everywhere. Even atheists can send out good vibes. So what if they don't believe in God? God still believes in them. There is the Buddhist practice of *tonglen,* where you breathe in the pain of the world, and breathe out love. Just as trees take in carbon dioxide and re-oxygenate the air, our prayers can raise the esteem of people everywhere — and all this rising esteem will undoubtedly improve the atmosphere!

And if you feel like you don't have a prayer, try these:

May the light of loving laughter radiate out to illuminate darkness everywhere, especially those poorly lit corridors of power.

May truth emerge from its hiding places, and healing balance be restored to every cell in the body politic.

May every born feed-us enjoy the right to laugh, and may freedom ring in the sound of every child's laughter.

★ TRULY UNBELIEVABLE

Shoot Out At the I'm-OK-You're-Not-OK Corral, or Welcome to the Disharmonic Convergence

*T*hey say God works in mysterious ways, but when it comes to working in mysteriously ungodly ways, you just can't beat human beings. Consider that we have the three major Middle Eastern religions laying claim to the same religious turf — a Holy War over the Holy Land. And factions of all three religions believe we're in the final minutes of the game — it's fourth down with inches to go, and each is hoping for a Completion in the End Zone.

Consider the history. The site in question, the Biblical Mount Moriah, was the site of both the Hebrews' First

Temple (destroyed by Nebuchadnezzar back in 586 B.C.), and the Second Temple, which the Romans took down in 70 A.D. According to Jewish tradition, the Messiah can come only when the Temple is rebuilt for the third time on the same site. Never mind the difficulty in getting insurance (hey, two major karma accidents in 2,600 years is definitely a blemish on your akashic record), there's another minor problem as well.

Seems the Muslims have had their eye on the same piece of property because the Prophet Mohammed used it as a launching pad for his eternal journey. In 685, the Muslims began to build the Noble Sanctuary, which contains the Dome of the Rock and the Al Aqsa mosque. But wait, there's more. To complete this disharmonic convergence, Christian Fundamentalists believe that the same piece of turf will be where the Battle of Armageddon is fought between the forces of the Antichrist and a 200-million man army from the East. Boy, talk about bad feng shui.

The Muslims have a slightly different story about the Battle of Armageddon. Their antichrist figure is a Jew named Dajal, who will lead a war against Islam, culminating in the return of Jesus as a Muslim prophet. Now any one of these movie scripts, should they ever make it to the screen, would make Mel Gibson's "Passion" look like "Pee Wee's Great Adventure." But there are people who believe with every high fiber of their beans in one of these scenarios, and they will fight to *your* death their right to believe it. So Jerusalem in the new millennium is like a very unfunny crowded stateroom scene in "A Night at the Opera," with each principal praying their fat lady sings first.

Breed It, and He Will Come . . . or, "Holy Cow!"

Now if you were to survey the Holy War in the Holy Land and exclaim, "Holy cow!" . . . you would be absolutely right. Because what's holding back building the Third Temple — aside from those pesky Muslims having claimed the area for *their* temple —

is that in order to set foot on the site, Jews must first be ritually purified, and in order for this purification to take place, not just any calf — but a red calf — must be sacrificed. Now a pure red heifer is apparently as rare as a purple cow, and no fair using artificial coloring. After all, how can you kill a calf that's already dyed?

Throughout history the Jews have tended to be fatalistic about the Messiah thing. Not so some fundamentalist Christians. They say, "Hey, if we can breed a red calf, we can *make* the Messiah come!" Never mind that it sounds like the young child vigorously wagging his dog's tail saying, "I want my dog to be happy." These folks are serious, and it has led to a "holy alliance" between a Catholic rancher in Nebraska, a Pentecostal minister from Mississippi, and an Orthodox rabbi in Israel to breed a literal sacred cow. No kidding.

They've all become friends, and it is certainly heartening to see a Protestant, a Catholic and a Jew working together to bring about the end of the world. However, to Muslims and non-messianic elements in Israel, this red calf is a red flag. Already, authorities have foiled messianic Jewish plots to blow up the Muslim's Dome of the Rock, an act that the Muslims would probably take with their characteristic good humor.

And already one "flawlessly red" calf was born, but alas before the proper age of sacrifice, it began to show a few white hairs. Another one is set to come of age next year, and if inspectors don't find any white hairs, there could be a whole lot of people seeing red. Now for those of us — the majority of people in the world, it turns out — who don't hold any of these messianic beliefs, it all seems like bull. It doesn't matter — sacred cow or profane bull, there are serious people intent on making the end of the world a self-fulfilling prophecy.

In a Shrinking World, Maybe What the World Needs is a Good Shrink

Back in the early 60s, Dr. Milton Rokeach, a resident psychiatrist at Ypsilanti State Hospital in Michigan, was faced with an intriguing situation. He had three mental patients who all claimed to be Jesus Christ. Back in those days, there were really no reality TV shows, except those panel game shows. And since this probably

47

would have been a little too edgy for "To Tell the Truth" ("My name is *Jesus Christ*." "*My* name is Jesus Christ." "My *name* is Jesus Christ."), he decided to do the next best thing. (No, not a sitcom called "My Three Christs." How could you even *think* something like that?) He put the three of them together in a therapy group — sort of a Candid Karma kind of a thing — and waited for the fun to begin.

In his book about the experiment, "The Three Christs of Ypsilanti" (it's really a book, you could look it up), Dr. Rokeach writes about how these three delusional characters accommodated — and did not accommodate — one another. And in the end, at least one of them suspected that maybe we're *all* Jesus Christ.

Fast forward about forty years and the experiment — or at least a version of it — continues. Only this time, the setting is Jerusalem and the three patients are Islam, Christianity and Judaism. Each, at its most extreme, lives in the delusional system that it alone is the One True Path. And unlike the Three Christs of Ypsilanti, these folks are armed and dangerous. And now, in the Mother of All Psychology Experiments, God has placed them in therapy together in a city that all three hold holy. Meanwhile, the rest of the world gets to see if the Big Three Karma Dealers can transcend their delusions enough to curb their dogmas instead of having them poop on someone else's sacred ground. Now *this* is what I call a reality TV show!

Now it may sound a little extreme — blasphemous even — to refer to sacred systems as "delusional", but Webster's doesn't lie. The dictionary defines "delusional" as a "belief held despite invalidating evidence." Now while there may not be any irrefutable evidence that invalidates any particular religious belief — unless, of course, you want to believe in the "junk sciences" of biology, archeology and anthropology — there is evidence that invalidates the childish notion, "my dogma's better than your dogma." It doesn't seem to matter what breed of dogma you've got, they all have the same Master.

Amazing True Facts: Science Proves Prayer Works, Even When Religion Doesn't!

In his book, "Prayer is Good Medicine," Dr. Larry Dossey cites numerous experiments where patients who are prayed for heal more quickly and have fewer complications following surgery. These experiments were done as serious double-blind experiments, and were repeated using animals (as the pray-ees, not the pray-ers), and the results were the same. It seems that all that was needed was a prayerful intention, and the prayer worked. No one religious system was shown to work better than another.

Pray-Back Time is Here

So, what can we conclude from this? Well, for one thing, next time you're sick, pray to be in the prayed-for group. But more importantly, the belief that one's own religious system is the One True Path ends up being the One True Pathology because evidence says any well-intentioned prayer works equally well.

Right now, elements in those three religions are sticking to their stories, and indeed the entire region remains littered with dogma-doo. But as more and more of their followers become leaders in telling the highest truth, maybe they'll end up like the more enlightened Christ of Ypsilanti, who put one and one and one together — and got One.

These religions, bless 'em, have provided us with spiritual nourishment for years, and we know that their prayers work. They have prayed for our souls. And now it is time for us to pray them back. Let us now pray for their Souls to rise together in levity, as they overcome the gravity that has brought them down — and threatens to take the rest of us down with them.

Time to Milk the Sacred Cow, and Take the Bull By the Horns

By now, you're probably ready for some good news, so here it is: There is no need to butcher anyone's sacred cow, if we just cut through the bull. Remember love vs. fear? The sacred cow is the milk of human kindness, which nourishes us. The bull is everything else. Those fighting dogmas, those pit bulls pitting their bull against someone else's, that is the bull we must take by the horns.

The bull is our stubborn addiction to mind and matter — usually in the form of rigid religious doctrine — when really it is the heart that matters. And at the heart of the matter is love. That is our source of Vitamin Be One. Think about it. While it is admirable when people use the Bible as a standard and go through every aspect of their life with a fine couth tome, having a one-tract mind has its limitations.

And while it is true that the unexamined life is not worth living, it is equally true that the unlived life isn't worth examining. Focusing more on the letter than the Spirit is like going into a fabulous restaurant — and chowing down on the menu.

So I say, when you find a sacred cow, milk it for all it's worth. How fortunate we are when we find a spiritual expression that — well, that gives us a heart on. Whatever that religion or spiritual path is, let's use it for goodness sakes!

Even if we don't know God, we all know Good. Just about everyone knows what it means to bring even just a small piece of goodness to the world. I mean goodness gracious, maybe if more people experienced loving arms, we wouldn't have rival groups each insisting God is with them, holding the rest of the world at armaments' length. Maybe we need to take this "born again" thing seriously — without reincarnation, that is. What if, in all our communities, we invited people (in any religion, in all religions, and in none) to experience being reborn into loving arms?

Maybe if we all rebirthed ourselves into this new world in this way, we would get that no matter where we reside on Spaceship Earth, we're all womb-mates. If more people were received by loving arms when they emerged from their womb, there would be fewer of us humans lovelessly arming.

But Seriously, Folks . . . What Would Gandhi Do?

Long, long ago the first pre-dominator who wanted to predominate realized that when it comes to getting another to bend to your will, all you need is fear. This idea caught on. And for millennia, we have had an inbred feariority complex that makes us susceptible to being remotely controlled just by someone pressing the fear button. And one of the prime symptoms of these feelings of feariority is irony deficiency.

If you want a graphic vision of what fearful people can do to an individual who preaches seeing beyond the fear, go see what happened to Jesus in Mel Gibson's "The Passion." And if you want an example of what fearful people with severe irony deficiency can do, consider the millions who were tortured (or for that matter, torched) by the church — in the name of Jesus, for Christ's sake!

A fitting follow up — one which would serve as a potent irony supplement to those who most need it — would be a 50 million hour sequel showing — in all its gory — all the witches, heretics, Jews, pagans and others tortured by a tortured, bass-ackwards interpretation of the Christ's loving message. When you watch the Pharisees portrayed in the movie calling out for Jesus' crucifixion, just picture some of the unfun fundaMENTALists of today who have crucified the true Christ energy a thousand times with their anti-love judgmentalism.

Some of those same people who rail so thunderously against the "abomination" of two men lying together in "sin", seem to have no problem when our own ruling cadre crawls into bed with evil dictators (yes, we set up both Saddam and Osama, you could look it up) and sinfully lies to convince us to "bomb a nation" like Iraq. Didn't hear Jerry Falwell or Pat Robertson raising a religious ruckus about this un-Jesus-like behavior.

Maybe it's time for Christian-identified folks who feel that to bomb a nation is the true abomination to begin to prod the Religious Right (aka "The Grinch Who Stole Christianity") with the question, "What would Jesus REALLY do?" If Jesus were a carpenter today, he would no doubt be driving a pick-up truck. But would he be brandishing a "God, Guns, and Guts" bumper sticker? I don't think so.

Maybe a better question for our times would be, "What would Gandhi do?" Hey, leave it to God to make the most Christian Christian since Christ a Hindu. Maybe we need an individual — or individuals — ruled by love and not fear to help all of us live up to our spiritual ideals.

Take those Palestinian suicide bombers— please. Here is my vision. As each enters the Gates of Heaven, God clops him on the head and says, "Schmuck! What'd you do that for? Just for that, instead of 72 virgins you get one 72-year-old virgin . . . and he answers to the name of Ayatollah." Think of the role models we've had for liberation over the past century. Not just Gandhi, but Nelson Mandela. The Dalai Lama. And the best they can come up with is murder-suicide? Where is Jack Kevorkian when you really need him?

And the Israelis? What if they did something really really odd and adopted a "no retaliation" policy instead of being drawn into the gutter of the lowest common dominator? Would there be more or fewer casualties than over the past four years? Or would this become the foundation for those on both sides willing to use their courage and fearlessness on behalf of peace?

What If We Practiced What They Preached and Made the Golden Rule the Golden Ruler?

*E*very year I do my State of the Universe Address, and every year it's pretty much the same thing. The Universe is doing fine, thank you, purring in perfection, humming along swimmingly, ever-changing as always. The state of the Universe . . . is sublime.

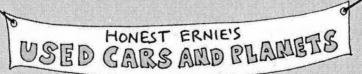

The state of our world . . . is sub-lemon. Indeed, we must wonder sometimes if there is some kind of Universal Lemon Law that will allow us to trade in this old beater of a karma for a shiny new one. Indeed, for centuries, good and well-meaning people have attempted to attune into Divine through various spiritual practices. And yet, despite all of our heavenly aspirations, we humans seem hell-bent on . . . hell.

Harry Cohen Baba was once asked if prayer healed everything, and he told the following Zen Cohen: For thirty years, a devout Jewish man would go to the Wailing Wall every day and pray for peace. Without fail, rain or shine, no matter what the circumstances, this dedicated man offered his prayer. A reporter from the Jerusalem Post found out about it, and interviewed the man. "I am truly impressed," she told him. "Tell me, what is it like going to the Wailing Wall every day for thirty years and praying for peace?"

"It's like talking to a &#$%&# wall!" he replied.

Yes, at some point there must be a transition from the metaphysical to the physical, so that the talkie-talkie becomes a walkie-talkie. At a time when loving kindness is so in demand, I recommend practicing supply-side spirituality in our daily doings. Now take those folks working ardently to grow the red heifer — I have no beef with them. But what if all that work and love and effort went into improving reality instead of ending it?

Help me with this one, please. If these people already know exactly how everything is going to turn out, why are they even bothering to live through it? I am reminded of an interchange between two enlightened teachers, the sportscaster Howard Cosell, and the baseball great Willie Mays. "We're talking with Willie Mays," said Howard. "Willie, lemme ask you this. Are you going to lead the league in homers again this year?"

And Willie Mays, with Yogi-like wisdom, replied, "I dunno, Howard. That's what we're gonna play the season to find out."

And what those of us who believe in Nonjudgment Day and Disarmaggedon are playing the season to find out is, can we create the field of dreams where the Messiah cannot help but show up? And wouldn't it be funny if, in the process of building the Messiah's natural habitat, we found out that we ARE the Messiah? Personally, I think the old time religions kind of missed the boat on this one. We are not here to earn God's love, we are here to spend it!

And what better way to spend it than mining gold and sharing it with all. While most of us weren't paying attention, alchemists quietly boiled every religion down to its essence, and what do you know? All of the essences are essentially the same. It all boils down to a variation of the Golden Rule: Do unto others as you would have them do unto you. And if you don't believe me, here is the same Golden essence expressed in eight different ways:

The Golden Rule Rules!

Buddhism. Hurt not others in ways that you yourself would find hurtful.

—Udana-Varga 5,1

Christianity. All things whatsoever ye would that men should do to you, do ye so to them; for this is the law and the prophets.

—Matthew 7:1

Confucianism. Do not do to others what you would not like yourself. Then there will be no resentment against you, either in the family or in the state.

—Analects 12:2

Hinduism. This is the sum of duty; do naught onto others what you would not have them do unto you.

—Mahabharata 5,1517

Islam. No one of you is a believer until he desires for his brother that which he desires for himself.

—Sunnah

Judaism. What is hateful to you, do not do to your fellow-man. This is the entire Law; all the rest is commentary.

—Talmud, Shabbat 3id

Taoism. Regard your neighbor's gain as your gain, and your neighbor's loss as your own loss.

—Tai Shang Kan Yin P'ien

Zoroastrianism. That nature alone is good which refrains from doing another whatsoever is not good for itself.
—*Dadisten-I-dinik, 94,5*

(Adapted from "The Christopher Newsletter")

Do you think they're trying to tell us something? What if enlightened religious leaders of the world said, "Let's cut the B.S., and make the Golden Rule our golden ruler." I say if we threw everything else away, and did just this, we'd do more than improve reality. We'd reap a world win!

SWAMI'S TELL A VISION
Blisskrieg Culminates in Pray-Offs; Worldwide Calm-Petition Draws Millions

I have a dream . . . that people from each and every spiritual path take seriously the idea of E Pluribus Unum — out of many, One, and in turn we create a yearly festival of prayer and celebration.

Jerusalem would be the perfect site for the God Will Games, or Pray-Offs if you prefer, and any spiritual path that wants to participate will be able to share its loving prayer. Although I am a firm advocate of nonjudgment, for this event we make an exception as judges from around the world rate each prayer for beauty, style, and overall magnificence.

In my dream, the event begins with the universal chant of "Om" so that we establish for everyone om-field advantage. Everyone is honored, even atheists (in their case, with periodic moments of silence). Everyone benefits from the event, and all monies raised go to ending spiritual hunger on the planet.

Meanwhile, I see the blisskrieg concept brought home to each and every community, where an Eternal Flame prayer circle is established. Any and every religion or spiritual discipline that wants to be represented can play and pray it forward, and the prayer is kept going day and night, like a flame that is never extinguished. Anyone who loves to pray is invited, and the prayer is for the happiness of all beings.

VIGIL AUNTIES

I'm seeing hordes of church ladies, old maiden aunts who love to pray, convening on universal prayer vigils in every town in America — vigil aunties, they are called. I see circles of people in prayer passing those cute little hug-a-planets and massaging whatever hot spot has flared of late. And there is plenty to heal: the ire in Ireland, the hurts in Herzegovina, the mess in Mesopotamia, the hate in Haiti . . . Will it help? I can't say for sure, but like chicken soup, it couldn't hurt.

Am I serious? No, but I used to be. In these serious times, the last thing we need is more seriousness. So these prayer sessions need to be joy-filled, so that all in the world can hear God's loving voice loud and clear. But I am serious about one thing. Should the God Will Games ever come about, I promise to be there to channel Howard Cosell doing the pray-by-pray.

SWAMI ANSWERS YOUR QUESTIONS . . . AND YOU WILL QUESTION HIS ANSWERS

The Angels Have Landed

Dear Swami:

With everything going on these days, one thing positive I notice is that there seems to be increased angelic activity on earth. Everywhere I go, I seem to see representations of angels, even on TV and in the movies. Have you noticed this too?

—Diane Gotuhevn,
Ballwyn, Missouri

Dear Diane:

Oh yes, the angelic realm is doing its part to make sure more and more humans are struck by enlightening during the ongoing blisskrieg. And by the way, the angels have upgraded and updated their entire system. Now, it's every time a cell phone rings, an angel gets his wings. The angelic energy is everywhere. Even Fox Network is coming up with an angel show, but you know how edgy Fox is. The show will be called "Inappropriately Touched By An Angel."

Want Peace? Meditation is the Answer

Dear Swami:

I read with interest that you participated in the worldwide meditation for peace several months ago. Do those things actually work? If so, where's the proof?

—Nora Spontz,
Louisville, Kentucky

Dear Nora:

Yes, it works and the results were extraordinary. During the entire duration of the meditation, there was not one act of violence perpetrated by anyone taking part. This is an amazing 100% success rate! The trick now is to get everyone on the planet meditating all the time.

Can Prayer Influence Outcome of a Sports Event?

Dear Swami:

My friend and I made a bet, and we thought you could settle it. He says, no way prayer can influence the outcome of a sports event. I say, "Way." Who's right?

—Boog Alou,
Bronx, New York

Dear Boog:

Tell your friend to pay up. Not only can prayer influence an outcome, it has. Remember back in 1999 when baseball player Manny Ramirez, who was then with the Cleveland Indians, had more runs batted in than anyone in nearly sixty years? Well, part of the credit has to go to some loyal Buddhist fans who attached themselves to the Indians because they thought they were from India. They would come to every Indians' home game, and each time Manny Ramirez came up with runners in scoring position, they would stand up and chant, *Oh Manny bat me home, Oh Manny bat me home, Oh Manny bat me home,* and quite often he did.

Meditation Works!

Dear Swami:

It would seem that with all the powerful group meditations being done these days, that someone would use meditation to help reduce crime in our cities. In fact, I seem to remember there was some kind of experiment a while back, but I don't remember hearing what the result was. Do you know anything about this, Swami?

—Sara Ann Rapp,
Midland, Michigan

Dear Sara Ann:

As a matter of fact, I know just what you're referring to. Several years ago, 2,000 meditators converged on Washington, D.C., a city long plagued by random and senseless crime. After six months of vigorous and focused meditation, I am happy to report, random and senseless crime was cut in half! For some inexplicable reason, however, pre-meditated crime was up sharply.

Holy War in the Holy Land? Holy Shit!

Dear Swami:

Don't you find it ironic that we have three major religions — coming from the same roots — who can't seem to agree how to create peace in . . . the Holy Land? Any signs of hope for peace in the Middle East?

—Donovan Newage,
Sebastopol, California

Dear Donovan:

Yes, it is ironic indeed when you stop to think about it: A Holy War in the Holy Land . . . Holy shit! It's a good thing they don't let you sue religions for malpractice, otherwise all those guys would have gone Chapter (and Verse) Eleven. Boy, talk about sects abuse! But being a hopeful optimystic, I believe we can and must send those bad dogmas to obedience school. Call it penance or call it a political science experiment, here's my idea:

Have the U.N. declare the Holy City of Jerusalem a "Pocket Protectorate," under the joint-jurisdiction of Christians, Muslims and Jews who believe in sects equality. And because this is declared Holy Ground for all, it's strictly shoes off. No street shoes, and no guns. To enter the Holy City, everyone must lay down their arms. Now they will look pretty funny with their arms on the ground and their butts sticking up in the air, but I tell you what. You cannot attack anyone in that position (unless, of course, you're adept at gastral projection).

To make it easier to let go of past grudges, the time in the Holy City will always be Now. Because, after all, if you're going to try something different, now is the time, right? Each and every pilgrim is free to walk the streets without fear or violence — because the U.N. says so, and because the rest of us took a stand for safe sects. Any dispute, they turn it over to the ombuddhasman. And if there is still conflict, they seek the highest perspective of all — levity. The Supreme Court Jester has the final say.

Now I am imagining this, and you may say I'm a dreamer. But I'm not the only one. Because already this idea is taking hold. I just heard about a new singing group made up of one Muslim, one Christian and one Jew. It's called Three Dogma Night. And anything that brings joy to the world is a good start.

Elvis Has Enlisted in the Blisskrieg

Dear Swami:

I guess I'm a seeker. I've tried on numerous religions, but none of them seem to fit. Right now I'm looking for something earthy yet soulful, transcendent and yet physical — but without too many commandments. Any ideas?

—Annie Mae Jerdude,
Birmingham, Alabama

Dear Annie Mae,

Well, have you considered becoming a Presleyterian? That's the Way of Elvis, and it's one of those new "lite" religions. Same satisfying flavor, and one third the commandments. For Elvis only asks three things of his faithful:

Love Me Tender.
Please Surrender.
Return to Sender.

It's very popular these days, especially in Las Vegas. Think of it. You see thousands and thousands of Elvis impersonators. How many Jesus impersonators have you seen? (Outside of mental hospitals, that is.)

Presleyterianism has something for everyone. The Orthodox Presleyterians put on their ritual sideburns every morning and do their salute to the sun singing, "Hunka Hunka Burnin' Love." Meanwhile, every Saturday evening the Elvis's Witnesses go door-to-door "Preslytizin" and asking people, "Are You Lonesome Tonight?"

Although he's been physically off the planet for more than twenty-five years, Elvis still takes a keen interest in the world — and boy is his business thriving! When I saw him this year at the Ascended Masters Golf Tournament, he told me he was very concerned about the state of the world, and he wanted to convey an urgent message for peace, to move the blisskrieg forward so that more and more people get struck by enlightening — because it's now or never:

A Channeled Message From Elvis: "It's Now or Never"

It's now or never
Though things seem tight
Blisskrieg my darlings
Be kind tonight
Tomorrow may be too late

It's now or never
Our peace won't wait.

Just when we reckoned
We had nearly ascended
Our White House was captured
Our karma, rear-ended
When terrorists frighten
Let our laughter enlighten
And poof goes the fear
The heart is clear at last

It's now or never
Though things seem tight
Blisskrieg my darlings
Be kind tonight
Tomorrow may be too late
It's now or never
Our love won't wait.

Ever since Adam
Munched on Eve's little apple
We've felt so guilty
We cried in the chapel
They call us sinners
But in love we are winners
Now love is here
The time for fear has passed

It's now or never
Though things seem tight
Blisskrieg my darlings
Beam love tonight
Tomorrow the world may cease
We don't have forever to hold our peace

Thank you very much, and hope to see y'all in Graceland . . .

The Real Key to the Universe

Dear Swami:

You've probably been asked this a million times, but I've got to know. What is the key to the Universe?

—Ewell Nevenoe,
Misty Point, North Carolina

Dear Ewell:

Well, I have bad news and good news. The bad news is, there is no key to the Universe. The good news is, it has been left unlocked.

But Seriously, Folks . . .

What if we practiced the one fun fundamental all religions preach? What if we enrolled in a One-Step Program to experience Oneness? Step One? Actually practice the Golden Rule. One for all, and all for One.

And once we've enrolled ourselves, let's become enrolling stones and enroll all of our government and public institutions to follow the Golden Rule. No killing, no stealing, and no perjury. What if each corporation had to hire an ombuddhasman to make sure they're doing everything by the Golden Rulebook?

What do we have to lose? In other words, why not go for heaven on Earth — just for the hell of it?

Tell-A-Vision

And Change the Programming for Good

*"If you don't like the current programming,
turn off your TV and tell a vision instead."*

I
f you don't like the current programming, here's a do-it-yourself
project that you can do yourself: Turn off your TV and tell a
vision instead. We all have a very clear and vivid picture of what
we don't want. It's all over the TV. Yep, we know what's pulling us
backward to the way it's always been. To move forward on the road
not yet traveled, we have to find out what is calling us forth. And
that is tell-a-vision. I tell a vision to you, you tell a vision to me,
and then we step into these happy, functional visions instead of
what we've been stepping into the past few millennia.

Tired of Reruns? Picture Something New

Here's the problem. Much of what we call "reality" is an out-picturing of our inner pictures, and many of our inner pictures are
simply reruns of the outer pictures we see every day. So if we want
to change the programming, we must get out from behind the
remote, tell our vision, and produce our own program.

Imagine a New Natural Anthem

For too long, humankind has been dreaming the impossible
dream, and it's worked. We've become impossible. So now it is
time for us to dream the possible dream and create some new possibilities. First thing is, let's transcend our old national anthems,
and create a *natural* anthem instead. We don't need to affirm

bombs bursting in air, and what's with these ram parts? Sounds pretty perverse, if you ask me. The only ones who should be concerned with ram parts are sheep. Seems to me we've been ramming parts for far too long. All of that unchecked male energy, all of those stags going at each other, that has caused a stag-nation. We need an Imagine-nation. And that is why I am pitching the song, "Imagine" as our new Natural Anthem — to help us get out of the rutting rut and imagine something different for a change.

★ TRULY UNBELIEVABLE

Imagine No "Imagine"

*I*n the days following 9/11, Clear Channel Radio — the most massive commercial radio media in America — wanted to make sure that its listeners were in the proper frame of mind, so they banned the song "Imagine" from their airways.

Never mind the irony deficiency of calling the greatest purveyor of mind-fogging right-wing talk radio "Clear Channel." But I guess when you're trying to clearly channel the body politic into a fearful frenzy imagination can be a pesky distraction. And I can see their point. Imagine how confusing it would be to be preparing for a war, and have to hear "imagine no possessions" or "imagine all the people living life in peace?"

While "Imagine" topped the list of banned songs (until Neil Young bravely restored it to the public ear at the benefit concert for 9/11 victims), there were many more dangerous tunes they didn't want playing in our heads.

Clear Channel's American Banned-Stand Top Fifteen

Now, it's understandable that these "inflammatory" songs (all of which were banned) might have been in bad taste:

Eve of Destruction
You Dropped The Bomb on Me
Hit Me With Your Best Shot
Great Balls of Fire
Burning Down the House
I Go To Pieces

But here are some, like "Imagine", which were dangerous because they might have caused some bleeding hearts to go soft around the edges:

Get Together
Morning Has Broken
Peace Train
He Ain't Heavy, He's My Brother
What a Wonderful World
War (What is it Good For?)
Spirit in the Sky (okay, I could see where this could have a double meaning)

. . . and finally two that were geographically undesirable:

New York, New York
Walk Like An Egyptian (no kidding, this was banned)

Crossing the Imaginot Line

Students of history — rare as they are nowadays — might remember that after World War I, which was the War to End All Wars for about twenty years — France decided that their best defense against Germany was to build a wall of fortification called the Maginot Line. Never in their wildest imagination could this wall be crossed or violated. Until it was.

Here in America, we have thought of freedom of speech, freedom of press, and freedom of imagination as inviolable rights protected by the Constitution. In our collective imagination, we have imagined the Imaginot Line that can never be crossed by anti-democratic forces, particularly in our own country. But to some people, the power of imagination, the power for us to imagine a better and different world, that indeed there is nothing above us but sky, is deeply threatening. And these folks think nothing of riding roughshod over the Imaginot Line — and doing unimaginable things to our right to imagine.

Here is the good news: In a world of scarcity (not to mention "scare city"), imagination is the most abundant resource we have. The more each of us becomes a clear channel by telling our own healing vision, the more likely Clear Channel is to channel our highest will and aspirations — or else fall on deaf ears.

But Seriously, Folks . . . Did You Know?

General Electric, which owns NBC, and cable networks MSNBC and Bravo, also manufactures engines for F-16 fighters, Apache helicopters, and Abrams tanks.

SWAMI'S TELL-A-VISIONARY DREAM
"Smart Planet, Foolish Choices"

Often, a telling vision begins with a dream, and here's mine. I dreamed that the Earth wasn't feeling well and went to see a doctor. "Doc," said the planet, "I'm feeling depleted. My water tastes funny, I have terrible-smelling gas, and there's this premature bald spot in my ozone layer. I figure I must be running some kind of fever, because I've been awfully warm lately. And I'm getting those tremors more often."

"Hmm," said the doctor. "About how long have you been having these symptoms?"

"Not long. Just for the past hundred years or so. But recently it's gotten worse, especially those violent flares up around my hot-spots."

"Well, you definitely show signs of mineral loss and lack of oxygen. You've been overmined, and consequently you've been undermined. Looks like you got a pretty nasty case of . . . People.

"People? Isn't that a benign condition?" the Earth asked.

"Well," replied the doctor, "it was, for many thousands of years. People lived in relative harmony with other organisms, and their numbers were kept in check. But there must have been some mutation because People are now the most dangerous parasite the Earth has ever known, consuming everything in sight, and leaving behind abnormal growth and toxic waste."

Naturally, the Earth wanted to know whether the condition is curable. "Yes, it is," the doctor said. "There's a warm solution anyone can make that will dissolve all toxicity. And that is —"

But I never finished the dream. Unfortunately, my hotel radio alarm was set to a radio talk show and I was abruptly awakened by somebody's barking dogma. All day I pondered the dream. Yes, it was clear that People were indeed the problem. For one thing, there's already too many of us, and more of us arrive every day. All it takes is for undulating and ovulating to occur at roughly the same time, and just like that you've sprung off some offspring. No wonder we are eating our host out of house and home.

And our petrochemical dependency has fouled the air. If he were alive today, Franklin D. Roosevelt would probably say: "We have nothing to fear, but atmosphere itself." And clear-cutting? It's clear-cut insanity! It's put us out on a limb, and we've continued cutting without noticing which side of limb we are sitting on.

That next night, I went back into the dream state with the intention of asking the Earth exactly what the doctor ordered. So naturally, I dreamed I was a talk-show host and had the Earth as my guest. I said, "You know, you're a pretty smart planet. But clearly, we humans have tried to outsmart you and have made some foolish choices. What do you suggest we choose instead?"

And the Earth replied, "Three things. Diversity, moderation and love." She elaborated on each of these, and I promised to convey her message to people everywhere. "Oh, and something else," the Earth told me, "I know that the military buzz cut has come back in style, but personally, I'm ready to let my forests grow long again. So I would appreciate it if you tell the folks that clear-cutting is no longer in fashion, thank you."

So, mea culpa. You-a culpa. We all a-culpa. Now what do we do it about it? We have been the problem and now it's time we applied the solution. Here is what the Earth suggested:

Diversity. The Earth was very upset about species loss and warned, "You are gambling with a paradise! What if I had put all my money on the dinosaur, where would we be today?" In diversity, we see that every species and indeed every individual is irreplaceable. I know this sounds odd, but each of us is one-of-a-kind. That's right. You are utterly unique — just like everyone else. When we truly get how extraordinarily odd each of us is, we will lose interest in trying to get even.

Moderation. The Earth has been fairly temperate, providing us with a pretty decent climate. But lately, with all the tempers flaring, the climate has become quite uncomfortable. We definitely need to moderate our consumption, and put our emotional energy to better use. Just think — if we channeled our frustration by practicing tantrum yoga, we could save energy by using our anger to heat our home in the wintertime. And with our anger released, we could live like nomads — that's where I nomad at you, you nomad and me, and consequently, there is no madness on the planet. When we live the nomad lifestyle, we are able to move more freely with a minimum of baggage — so we use up fewer resources.

Love. That was the part of the dream that I missed. Love is the solution that dissolves all of our problems. So here is the doctor's prescription: Every evening at sunset, dissolve all the stresses of the day in a warm solution of love. And at sunrise, do the same to dissolve all fears and anxieties. Feel all the love in the Universe seeping into every pore — like a good, cleansing esteem bath. Once you have bathed in the warm glow of the loving presence, now let it out to radiate everywhere. Jesus said, "Love thy neighbor as thyself," and maybe now is the time to launch a blisskrieg the likes of which the world has never seen. It's a question of evolution: Can mankind treat man kindly? There's no better time to find out.

Mother Earth First!

If we want our healing dreams to come true, we must first cultivate our field of dreams, which just happens to be the Earth we stand on. We've become so preoccupied and distracted by the War on Terror that we've barely noticed the War on Terra that has been going on for centuries, and that has particularly heated up (literally!) only recently.

Hey, if it's one area where we're living in the now, it's in using up the world's resources. In fact, when it comes to consumption we've gotten way ahead of ourselves. We're not waiting for the future. No sirree, we're brought the future into the here-and-now by consuming as much of it as we can. In fact, we can say our planet is dying of consumption.

Now there are those who say that our current administration hasn't lifted a finger for the environment, but that is not completely true. The middle finger is still a finger, is it not? And as a goodwill gesture to environmentalists, President Bush brought a special gift for his 'tree-hugger friends" from his ranch in Crawford, Texas — a prickly-pear cactus. In fact, his is a simple and time-honored policy for dealing with environmental destruction and global warming. When things get too hot, simply move somewhere else.

What do you think this idea of putting a man on Mars is all about? Well, we've about used up this planet. Time to move on to greener — I mean redder — pastures. The E.T.s certainly aren't pleased. The day the Mars probe landed, the headline in the Intergalactic Gazette was, "There goes the neighborhood."

As if we needed more Mars energy at this time. How come you never hear about putting a woman on Venus? Maybe the best way to heal the "stag-nation" that has caused us to believe that the Earth and all of her creatures are to be dominated by man-unkind, is to allow the feminine energy to make a doe-nation. In many Native American societies, for example, the decision to go to war rests finally with the grandmothers.

Instead of listening to the visionaries, the divisionaries in our current administration — empty warheads, I am sad to say — went off into Iraq half-cocked, got their Iraqs off, but haven't figured out how to get the Iraqis off of offing us. And I'm afraid there is a lot more offing in the offing in this awful movie, the Iraqi Horror Picture Show. For indeed the seizure of Iraq has turned out to be a grand mal seizure.

Maybe we need a no nonsense Grand*ma* — Granny D would fit the bill — to say, "The children need shoes. So there is no way you're goin' out with the boys, gambling on that good-for-nothing war, and shooting your wad! You bring that $107 billion back home right now, young man, or you're marching right back to Crawford, Texas — and no state dinner for you!"

Shift Happens!

A recent poll shows that a majority of Americans feel "confused" — and the rest "aren't sure." And no wonder. Times of great change are also times of great uncertainty. For example, have you heard of Heisenberg's Uncertainty Principle? Well, now they're not even sure about that.

Many, many mystics ("opti-" and "pessi-" alike), point to this period as a time when a great shift will take place. Now before we throw up our hands in horror and lament, "Why is this shift happening to me?" perhaps we'd do better by seeing it as a great opportunity. As a great Yogi once said, "When you come to a fork in the road, take it." And with so many paths spread out before us, what an opportunity to take the road not yet taken — and before the shift hits the fan, I might add.

Now of course, we fear upheaval, but I will tell you something. Compared to downheaval, upheaval is the lesser of two heavals. Sometimes when we are heaved upward, we rise high enough to see with a bigger perspective, and that in itself can keep us from plunging into the depths of downheaval. Of course, the ideal is for us to change our heaval ways, and vision and imagination hold the key.

If change is inevitable, why not get on the bandwagon ahead of the band? And if our leaders fail to lead, well then it's time for the bandwagon to start waggin' the band for a change. And let's do it before the nefarious band who've put themselves in charge bans band-waggin' completely.

Time for a New Reality TV

Do we really create our own reality? Or is it all scripted out over at Universal Studios? The debate has raged as long as debates have been the rage, and I can provide no definitive answer either. Certainly some really big blockbusters have come out of Universal recently — and more disasteroid scenarios are predicted for the near future. And yet, small independents continue to write and star in their own successful movies.

As more and more of these alternative scripts get produced, this is helping to bring about an *alter native* reality. And that is a good thing. For, indeed, the native reality could use some altering. In a recent reality check, 71% of those responding said they "disapproved" of the current reality — the lowest approval rating reality has had since the Great Flood. This is understandable. Consider the political scene, for goodness sakes. All those endless buttals and rebuttals. The media baits us into arguing, and we keep falling for debate. It is so silly — we could be making a beautiful brainchild together, and instead we are mass-debating.

If you don't like the current trance, tell a vision that can transform the trance. Instead of being just another divisionary taking sides on the latest televised drama, you can choose to become a visionary who uses these spectacles to help us all see more clearly. If enough of us do this, even mainstream media will have to replace its commentators with uncommontators who have an alter native vision. For indeed there is a Divine Order. When you tell your vision, you are filling out your Divine Order Form. As Harry Cohen Baba told us after one of his New Deli pilgrimages, "Life is like a good deli. If enough people order something — even if it isn't on the menu — they'll *have to* make it."

Tired of the "Survivor" programming? Let me tell a healing vision that might heal the television. How about a new reality TV show called "Thrivor"? A group of diverse strangers are stranded together on a small island (or, for that matter, a large country or medium-sized planet), and they must use their similarities and differences to work together. And if they succeed, they all win the prize. And those of us watching at home, we have a chance to root for everyone. Who knows? Maybe this is the kind of healthy programming that can reprogram the planet.

Create Global Heartwarming By Generating Esteem

I've said it before. It all boils down to which belief system we invest in. Do we feed our healthy and nourishing Belief in Good, or do we invest our precious energy in divisionary squabbles? Do we milk the sacred cow, or empower the bull? Every word we utter to another is a significant utterance that will either improve reality, or set us back into dueling dualities.

Part of the shift that is set to take place is shifting our karmas into higher gear. No longer do we have to fuel our karmas by internal combustion, which is getting more and more costly, not to mention the wear-and-tear on the parts. Can you imagine a world of clean-burning karmas run on esteem? Well, that vision can become a reality only if we ourselves become esteem-generators.

Yes, each of us at some time in our lives has been flattened by an esteem-roller, and it's taken months or years to get back up to a full head of esteem. You can speed up this process — and alter our native reality — by becoming an empowerhouse who helps others generate their own esteem. As you know, esteem rises and rising esteem might even be the cause of this global heart-warming we've heard so much about. People are definitely becoming warmer. Just a few years ago, it wasn't cool to be warm. Now being warm is becoming cool again. This is bound to have an effect on the overall climate.

★ PROFILES IN ENCOURAGEMENT

Swami's Tell-A-Vision for Reaping a World Win

*S*peaking of the overall climate, if this global warming continues unabated, it'll be too warm for overalls. And if we humans continue devouring the Earth's resources at the current pace . . . well, we might end up like those insects playing swallow the leader. The good news is, every crisis holds a new opportunity. So to kick off an entirely new season of programming, I have volunteered to tell my vision first:

Imagine renewable, sustainable, nonpolluting energy so abundant that we need no army to defend it. Remember the Manhattan Project where we focused all of our resources on creating the first weapon of mass destruction? This would be the Manhelpin Project, the ultimate weapon of mass construction that would end the need for war once and for all. Imagine all the peoples of earth working together as a team, playing a game where everyone wins. We'd have a healthy income, and a healthy outcome — what could be better?

And here is even more good news. Such a project already exists.

THE APOLLO ALLIANCE FOR NEW CLEAR ENERGY
"Finally, the Blues Stick With the Greens, So the Greens Don't Get Stuck With the Blues"

It used to be that getting blue-collar workers and environmentalists together on the same issue was like — well, it was like herding Democrats. But no more. Thanks to a forward-thinking organization called the Apollo Alliance, environmentalists and union members are working together on their version of the "Manhelpin Project." The Apollo Alliance is a "Manhattan Project" for developing renewable nonpolluting energy sources so that the United States becomes the worldwide leader in renewable technology.

This means better-paying, high tech jobs. And a cleaner environment. It's like those old beer commercials. "Great taste!" "Less filling!" Only this time it's, "Great jobs!" "Less polluting!" And the Teamsters Union and Sierra Club are actually on the same side! Now that the blue-collar folks get the economic power of green energy, and are sticking with the Greens, the Greens aren't stuck with the blues. After all, the best way to counter the divide-and-conquer strategy of the Banana Republicans is the unite-and-conquer approach.

The plan — which every Democratic candidate who ran in the primaries endorsed — involves a $300 billion investment over ten years (less than what we spend on the military in one year) to use American ingenuity and imagination to generate true wealth instead of killing people (and the environment) over dwindling fossil fuels. Indeed, here is a visionary idea for a change: High-paid, highly-skilled enviro-tech jobs that cannot be exported to develop new clear energy — wind, solar, geothermal, hydrogen, hybrid.

Imagine — creating a million jobs here where something clean is being produced, and at the same time creating an exportable technology that can help third world countries. While the original Apollo Project sought to have a human being walk on the moon, this one will insure that in twenty or thirty or fifty years, there will still be human beings walking on the earth.

Four Out of Five Transcendentists Recommend Mental Floss to Prevent Truth Decay

If you want clarity of vision, you need clarity of mind. And how can we have clarity of mind when we are being assaulted by massive amounts of information that can overwhelm even the most insatiable infomaniac? No wonder truth decay is rampant! And even though we all know it, most of us simply don't remember to use mental floss daily. It's such a simple solution. Each time you watch TV, listen to talk radio, or get inundated with crap coming from your own mind, just stop. Take a deep breath. Place your hands about six inches from each ear, and with an imaginary thread, begin a back-and-forth movement to clear out all of the unnecessary debris.

Feel those thought-particles dissolving, leaving your mind free and clear — without harmful brainwashing. You know all of that irrelevant or downright toxic information that needs to go in one ear and out the other? Now it can. This is particularly important for those of us who have been to school and have had our heads filled with extraneous "flossophy." Daily flossing will remove it, making your mind a vacuum that will suck in completely new thoughts!

But even with daily flossing, we all still need a trip to the transcendenist every now and then. And to make home care complete and effective, I have now come up with the ultimate meditation tape.

What Is the Sound of No Hands Clapping?
Swami's Ultimate Meditation Tape Will Clear Your Mind and Feed Hungry Children at the Same Time!

I am often asked, "How do you explain the suffering of those who do not have enough to eat?" And I answer that that is very easy to explain. What is harder to explain is the suffering of those who have too much to eat. We fill ourselves up with so many things because we think being filled full will lead to fulfillment. But that full feeling isn't fulfilling, is it? It only leads to emptiness, which is good. Because as Buddha told us centuries ago, nothing will make you happy.

And that is why my ultimate meditation tape, *The Sound of Silence,* is completely blank. Think about it. Our minds are filled up with information everywhere we go. After a busy day thinking of everything, what a welcome relief it is to think of nothing. And by the way, my *Sound of Silence* meditation tape is chock full of only the purest, highest quality nothing. We start with the most pristine silence from the quietest peak in the Himalayas. Then, this silence is premeditated by 1,000 Tibetan monks. And if that

isn't enough, we filter it through the finest sound filters on the planet. Believe me, if you hear anything while listening to this tape, it is completely in your head!

But wait — there's less! Because now you can satisfy your spiritual hunger and another's physical hunger at the same time!

Here's How You Can Help Feed Hungry Children — and Get Nothing in Return!

Now of course, we would never dream of charging money for this valuable tape. Oh, no. We are giving nothing away, because everyone knows that in this materialistic world, nothing is free. Just go to Swami's Om Page at www.wakeuplaughing.com and download as much silence as you can handle — absolutely free! A strict nothing for nothing deal. But I must tell you we are not giving away nothing for naught. There is a purpose. You know how people say that nothing will end hunger on the planet? Well, I am determined to prove them right. So when you come to my web site to download this remarkable healing silence, you will have a chance to donate money to feed hungry children. Because even though nothing is free . . . food costs money. And be sure and download a copy for everyone you know. Yes, nothing is too good for your friends — but get it for them anyway.

(Seriously folks. You can go to the website, download a everything from a moment of silence to a longer meditation, and "click for hunger." Try it.)

I know what you're thinking. Doing something for nothing? Nothing doing! But I say you will be restoring balance on the planet. Think about it. In some parts of the world, nothing is so abundant, that people eat it for two to three meals a day! Meanwhile, back here in the hustle and bustle of civilization, a moment of pure, sweet, unadulterated silence is as rare as a quarter-pounder in Bangla Desh.

The Silent Meditation Tape
People Can't Stop Talking About!

But never mind Bangla Desh. Here's what people like yourselves are saying about the *Sound of Silence* Ultimate Meditation Tape:

"All my life I have stopped at nothing in my quest for success and happiness. What a waste of energy! If only I had stopped at nothing and stayed there, I'd be peacefully waiting for everyone else."

—Anna Cheever,
Scarsdale, New York

"For the past several years, I've spent most of my time in front of my computer screen, playing video games and cruising the internet. My parents have scolded me for being a good-for-nothing. Well, thanks to your web site, I can not only BE good-for-nothing, I can click onto the hunger site and actually DO good for nothing. Just want to let you know that even a good-for-nothing can be good for something!"

—Horace Zontal,
Los Gatos, California

"I recently played your healing silence tape at the National Speakers Association convention. It left everyone speechless. I tell you, it was so quiet you could hear an opinion drop."
—Frieda Mind,
Elizabeth, New Jersey

And finally, an anonymous quote from one of our biggest success stories:

"No comment."

So Why Wait For Nothing? Unleash the Hidden Power of Nothing In <u>Your</u> Life Right Now

Yes, in these stressful times when we are inundated with disturbing sound bites, what a welcome release to experience the peacefulness of a soundless bite! Yum! And by the way, these tapes are completely safe for everyone, even children. Go ahead — meditate your head off! It can't hurt.

So why follow the herd, when you can follow the unheard instead? Go to Swami's Om Page at www.wakeuplaughing.com, download as much healing silence as you can handle, and take the opportunity to give something to someone who already has plenty of nothing — it's the least we can do.

SWAMI ANSWERS YOUR QUESTIONS . . .
AND YOU WILL QUESTION HIS ANSWERS.

The Past — There's Just No Future In It

Dear Swami:

I just finished reading that wonderful book, "The Power of Now". It all made sense to me, but I keep getting drawn back into regrets about the past. Someone recommended getting a past life reading, and it worked. Now I have regrets about my past lives as well. Swami, is there any way I can make peace with my past, and be in the "now" more?

—**Bea Fareel,**
Scarsdale, New York

Dear Bea:

I understand completely how difficult it is to be in the now. As soon as the thought runs through your mind, "Wait a minute, I think I'm in the now," it's too late. It's already then. Nonetheless, we are meant to be in the present time. Each moment, we are presented with a present, and if we're all caught up in the past, our presents remain unopened. So first, let's deal with past lives. I suggest you adopt my attitude: Past lives? Been there, done that. As for the more recent past, nothing works better than the peace mantra to put the past to rest. Next time an old trouble bubbles to the surface, just say the mantra, "Ah, PEACE ON IT!" You will release the past piece by piece. And each time you let go of a piece of the past, you will find more peace in the present.

Psychics Will Become Unnecessary, Swami Predicts

Dear Swami:

Are you psychic? And if so, what do you see in the cards for our world in the next year?

—Rhoda Ruder,
Redondo Beach, California

Dear Rhoda:

People ask me all the time if I am psychic, and I always give them the same answer: I knew you were going to ask that question. And yet, I am loath to make predictions for several reasons. First, i don't want to jeopardize my non-prophet status. If you are reading this book, you have probably paid money for it, and some of that money will make its way back to me. The Eternal Revenue Service has made it pretty clear that making predictions for money is a no-no. Propheteering, they call it.

The second reason I'm unwilling to make predictions is

because now they're taking psychics to court for malpractice. If I make a prediction and it doesn't come true, I can be sued. In other words, if you're a sucker for a seer, and what the seer sees sucks, you can redress your grievance in a seersucker suit.

But you know, the most important reason I don't make predictions is because this is indeed a universe of infinite possibilities, and anything can happen. They try to predict the weather, and one little butterfly fart can change everything.

So if we want truly unpredictable and unrecognizable results, my advice is close your predictionary, and turn on your tell-a-vision. Attune yourself to the clearest channel you can receive, and tell your vision to others. Then, put yourself into that picture. Live into that possibility until it becomes a probability. I predict that will lead to a future that is much healthier than the one we are currently plunging fool-speed ahead into.

Exploring Space on Five Dollars A Day

Dear Swami:

Is space our final frontier? And what are your feelings about extra-terrestials?

—Hugh Briss,
Lexington, Kentucky

Dear Hugh:

I have very strong feelings about extra terrestials. We already have way too many terrestials. We don't need any extra. And that is why the space issue is so important, because the more of us there are, the less space we seem to have. Einstein said that a problem cannot be solved at the level it was created, and this certainly makes sense to me. Surely we can't solve the problem of overpopulation by creating more people. Nor does it make a lot of sense to revert to the good old-fashioned ways of controlling population — war, disease, starvation — which certain old-time religions prefer to birth control.

The outer space solution, while attractive, is a bit dicey. I've been there, and I'll tell you one thing. The E.T.s I know are too hip to sell their planet for $24 worth of shiny trinkets. For another thing, there's the expense — even with all the technological breakthroughs. For example, I just read about plans to make currency out of a new space-age material that will allow the dollar to stretch a lot further. Spendex, it is called. But even with this unbelievable development, we will be stretched pretty thin.

That is why I say the real frontier lies in exploring inner space. With no more land to mine, we must now mine the mind for yet unimagined solutions. Yes, the unmined mind is our greatest resource. So let's make sure the mind is not undermined by toxic, limiting thoughts. I have often said that each of us already has all of the answers within. Have fun matching them with the corresponding questions.

Say It Forward

Dear Swami:

I think your idealism is a wonderful sentiment, but I'm concerned with the real deal. How much impact can these ideas really have? What can one person do?

—Javier K. Kaneetit II,
El Cajon, California

Dear Javier:

What can one person do? What about Mahatma Gandhi? Martin Luther King? Dr. Jonas Salk? Mother Teresa? George Gribblemyer? Oh, you haven't heard of George Gribblemyer? That's because HE DIDN'T DO ANYTHING!

Yes, part of turning the ideal into the real deal and

getting your script produced is, you have to speak it into existence. Think about it. If a lie repeated over and over is believed, what about the truth repeated over and over? Well, here are some ways you (and anyone you know), can say it forward and put your tell-a-vision program out on the networks:

1. Tell-A-Person. In this cyber-age where so much information is circulated on the internet, take it to the outer-net. Speak your truth clearly and calmly everywhere you go. When people disagree with you, make sure you disagree agreeably. If what they are saying sounds ridiculous, ask them to kindly repeat it. Who knows? With enough hearings, it might start sounding ridiculous to them too.

2. Coin and Circulate Your Own Words. If you think that words cannot describe the current state of insanity, think again. They can. When we coin words and put them into circulation, we pass along seeds of new ideas. These are called "memes," and they are most definitely memes to a higher end. If you need new words to pass along, look at Swami's Dictionary at the end of this book.

3. Reframe the Negative in a Positive Light. As my guru Harry Cohen Baba used to say, "Life is like photography. We use the negative to develop." So, if you find yourself knee-deep in you-know-what, look for the pony hidden in the picture. For example, those corporate wrongdoers from Enron who are concerned about going to jail should look on the bright side. They'll be living in a gated community.

4. Become Radioactive. If you have no one who'll listen to you, call your favorite (or better yet, your un-favorite) talk radio show, and talk back. Why? Well, for one thing if it's a highly rated show, you know someone is listening. Inundate right wing talk radio with wacky solutions out of left field. Make Rush Limbaugh laugh. Make everyone else think. Turn those dittoes over their heads into question marks.

But Seriously, Folks . . .

In this Universe of infinite potentials, do you think we could pos-sibly find a better future than the one the Banana Republicans are selling . . . endless warfare, environmental destruction, loss of civil liberties, growing gap between rich and poor?

Don't you wonder if there is a way we can use our infinite resource — imagination — to impact the finite resources on our planet?

Remember, the first and key step toward improving reality is having an out-picturing of a good picture, an alter native future where we natives are altered for the better.

Invest in A-Bun-Dance, Not Scare-City

How to Feed Two Birds With One Scone, and Make the Commonwealth Uncommonly Wealthy

*"Let's put our money into goods and services
instead of bads and disservices."*

O f all of God's creations facing extinction, perhaps the most serious threat is to our "common wealth." For if this splendid planet is indeed the Creator's creation then it belongs to no one . . . and to everyone. Together we the people of the world get to share — and manage — the common wealth for the common good of all.

Overmining Has Undermined Our Commonwealth

And the one practice that is most endangering our common-wealth is mining. That is when those who already have too much money and power take over and say, "This is mine, this is mine, this is mine." Now this mining has gone on ever since the first brute used brute strength, and now our planet is overmined, and the vitality of the body politic undermined. Think about it. Those peons get tired of being peed on. Forget trickle down. You get pissed on, you're gonna get pissed off. This leads to uprisings, which lead to downfalls, and all of this uprising and downfalling can be hard on the body politic — and expensive.

That's why the Gross National Product is so . . . gross. Because along with all of those goods and services, there are plenty of bads and disservices — all of the things needed to keep unhealthy "mining" operations going, and to deal with the inevitable uprisings and downfallings.

Which Future Are We Buying?

So we say, support the "alter native" economy — anything which alters us natives of Earth for the better. Let's start measuring the Net National Product, that which creates lasting value and uses uncommon sense to make the commonwealth uncommonly wealthy. Instead of piling up weapons and investing in insecurities, let's vote with our dollars and say, "Sorry, we're just not buying it." Everyone is selling futures nowadays, so let's choose the future we buy wisely. Studies show there are at least 50 million Americans who prefer to feed the wolf of peace. If each of us shifted just $100 from supporting the "gross" national product into the alter native economy, that would be $5 billion. Now that's just a drop in the bucket, but hey — it's a start.

No Privatizing Without Mutual Consent, Please

And let's stop this trend toward privatization of our God-given natural resources. We have to insist that those big, powerful companies stop using force to stick their privates where they don't belong. In any case, there must be mutual consent. I don't know about you, but where I come from, when you "privatize" people against their will, that is called rape. And when you do it to Mother Earth — well, there is a very impolite term for people like that.

Time for Corporations to Incorporate Personhood

As for the issue of corporate personhood, I can't understand how those Banana Republicans being so imbedded as they are with the Religious Right can actually support this notion of artificial life. Heck, in most places, these artificial entities have more rights than real people! So I say, if these corporations want human rights, they must have a human heart. I recommend that corporations applying for "personhood" must show evidence of a heart transplant (that's transplanted in, not out) and hire an ombuddhasman to make sure that the heart is always in command.

Vote for ABUNdance, Not Scare City

Finally, we the people must decide whether we feed the wolf of love with our dollars or the wolf of fear. Every monetary exchange is a vote. So we say, vote for "a bun dance" — that is where we all get up off our assets, move our buns, and dance together — instead of buying into the "scare city" currently being sold.

★ TRULY UNBELIEVABLE

Huge Drug Deal Goes Down
While America Looks the Other Way

While our government was busy telling our youngsters to just say no to drugs, Congress and the President were saying "yes, yes, yes" to the world's most notorious drug dealers. In 2003, in the guise of providing prescription drug benefits to Medicare recipients, Congress and the President happily dropped a $400 billion bundle at the feet of the international drug cartel. While the legislation will enable more seniors to pay more for drugs, it fails to address the real problem which is . . . paying more for drugs. Under this drug deal gone bad, drug companies will be able to pad their already-huge profits, and determine the bottom-line issue of who gets what life-saving drug strictly on the basis of their own bottom line. Boy, talk about making a killing.

And to get conservative Republicans who still believe in the old-fashioned notion of fiscal fitness to go along with this big payoff, the Administration lied about the actual cost, and threatened to fire an Office of Management and Budget official if he told anyone. Meanwhile, with a Republican majority in Congress, the Administration approached the American Association of Retired Persons (AARP), and told them that this is the best they could get and they'd better go along.

And so the AARP went "Aarp!" and swallowed the bitter pill. And we the people bought the farm, because the PhRMA bought the Congress.

PhRMA, for those who don't know, is the Pharmaceutical Research and Manufacturers Association, the industry lobbying group that has waged an effective and expensive campaign to get our legislators strung out on drug money. Consider the following truly unbelievable stats:

✓ The drug industry spent $97 million in 2000 on lobbying. With 535 members of Congress, that comes out to $181,308.41 worth of leverage applied to each one.

✓ They employ over 600 paid, full-time lobbyists — about 1.2 for every member of Congress. In other words, they can go one-on-one and still have some reserves on the bench.

✓ More than 50% of these lobbyists have a "revolving door" relationship with government, meaning they've worked in the past for Congress or other government agencies.

✓ Drug companies are the most profitable of all industries. In 2000, profit margins in the industry were nearly four times the Fortune 500 average.

✓ Drug companies actually spend just one fifth of what they say they spend on research and development for new drugs. While they claim to spend $500 million to bring a new drug to market, the real figure is more like $110 million.

✓ If that isn't enough taxing misrepresentation, they spend millions on advertising as extra "lie-ability insurance." One of their ads against generic drugs showed photos of sick children and weak seniors to suggest that generic drugs would make them worse. Not that there's any real evidence of that, but when you have hype and spin who needs evidence?

It's just a couple of seniors heading to Canada to buy drugs.

Their current campaign is to make sure Americans — particularly the elderly — don't make an end run and buy their drugs from Canada, where prices on many drugs are a fraction of what they are here. Last year, Vermont women were able to go north and purchase the widely prescribed breast cancer drug Tamoxifen at one tenth of the price that it sells for in the United States. The drug companies are trying to put an end to this un-American practice of "offshoring" drug purchases, and they're doing all this with money they're getting from you! Here's how well their strategy has paid off so far:

√ In 1999, drug companies made $7.3 million in direct campaign contributions.

√ The same year, the top ten drug companies averaged $2.5 billion (that's billion, folks) in profits.

√ Also that same year, they were able avoid $3.8 billion (again, billion) in taxes.

Indeed, drug company addiction has already caused irreparable damage to the body politic, and clearly it is up to we the people to check our legislators into a program — or else, turn these addicted dopes out of office.

Representation Without Taxation is Taxing the Body Politic

Boy, it seems like only yesterday American upstarts were railing against "taxation without representation." It's taken us over 200 years, and what do you know? The tax tables are completely turned. We now have representation without taxation, where some of the most influential corporations get to live offshore and pay little or no taxes. So not only have our jobs been outsourced, so has our government.

Welcome to the American Devolution. Now before you go blaming the usual devils for this devolutionary devilishness — those Banana Republicans and their gold collar criminal cohorts — we have to face the truth. After all, this is a 7-Step program and we seven-steppers say we have to tell the truth every step of the way. And to tell the truth, it all happened while we weren't paying attention. The day that President Ronald Reagan fluffed the body politic by declaring "Morning in America" — and began dismantling the people's systems of redress and recourse — it was really "mourning in America" for government of the people, by the people and for the people.

Less government and fewer regulations, that was the spin. Sounds a lot better than, "Less money and resources to protect we the people from gold collar criminals disguised as legitimate businesses."

With the federal government winking and nodding, many industries have concluded that when it comes to spending money, it's more efficient to eliminate the middle-man. Forget taxes. Let's just pay the legislators directly. We'll put our money into lobbyists who used to be legislators so they can grease the skids with the legislators who used to be lobbyists. And that, my friends, is how a democracy becomes a mockracy.

And these lowered taxes are a double-edged plowshare for corporations. Not only do they get to pay less in taxes, but because there's less tax money at work, there are fewer resources to enforce regulations — or for that matter, collect money. Even the IRS. They're so taxed by the lack of taxes that they don't even have the money to go after what they're owed!

Many of the world's largest companies pay no corporate income tax, and yet have more say than any million of us when it comes to what becomes law. Consider what these telling statistics are telling us about the taxing toll on the body politic:

√ The tax rate on capital gains, the source of more than half the income for the super rich, was 28 percent in 1987, was reduced to 20 percent in 1998, and then lowered again to 15 percent in 2003.

√ During the Eisenhower era (remember when moms didn't *have to* work?), corporations were responsible for one third of federal revenues. By 2002, it was down below 10%.

√ In 1977, the richest one percent of Americans had as much to spend after taxes as the bottom 49 million. By 1999, the top one percent had as much as the bottom 100 million Americans.

√ Between 1977 and 1999, those in the top one percent saw their income — in real dollars, and after taxes — double.

√ Meanwhile, the 55 million Americans in the poorest fifth of the population had their income fall from an average of $10,000 in 1977 to $8,800 in 1999.

√ In 1970, the poorest one third of Americans had more than ten percent of all income, the super rich had one percent. By 2000, the groups were equal — the 28,000 Americans at the top had as much income as the 96 million at the bottom.

No matter how much spendex you use, you can only stretch a dollar so far. And so far, for far too many, the dollars are too few and too far between. Just as the American patriots had to face the issue of taxation without representation 225 years ago, today American Evolutionaries must confront this issue of representation without taxation, and recognize that once again we are being colonized. It is time for we the people to just say no to the unhealthy colonic that is siphoning off our common wealth and overtaxing our system.

No wonder the powers that be in power want to classify any objection to this sorry state of affairs as "class warfare." Indeed, the war on poverty is over, and the poor people have been soundly defeated. Now the war has begun on the rest of us.

Serf City, Here We Come?

Yes, there is genuine concern that the next generation may grow up listening to serf music, as the world devolves into futile feudal feuds. But we American Evolutionaries have elected to tell the truth, and so let us look at some current fiscal disorders of the body politic, and how we might restore not just fiscal fitness, but vibrant good health.

The Military Industrial Complex

The Military Industrial Complex is perhaps the most deadly and debilitating psychological disorder a body politic can suffer from, a delusional state where sufferers continue to fight the Cold War, long after Cold War symptoms have subsided. And with no Cold War, thanks to this disorder, they've managed to heat up some hot wars, and even increase global warming in the process. Worse than that, the Military Industrial Complex — while a psychological condition — has had some severe fiscal consequences.

As with many imbalances of the body politic, the Military Industrial Complex we now suffer from started out as a healthy safeguard to defend against harmful and invasive foreign bodies. But with nothing to counterbalance its ravenous appetite, it's become a toxic, all-consuming parasite that continues to grow in the darkness and steal nourishment from healthy cells in the body politic. As a result, we have overdeveloped musculature (based on plenty of steroid use, believe you me) masking a deep heartsickness.

Furthermore, this parasite is actually feeding on the past and the future at the same time. Since the Military Industrial Complex thrives on fossil fuels, the fossilized fools in charge have charged ahead charging everything — to be paid by future generations. The problem is, the future is coming up very quickly — and the dinosaurs are coming home to roost.

Congressional Greedlock and Gold Collar Crime

Meanwhile, Congress — supposedly representing you and me — is stuck in greedlock. Seems as if the greedy parties have a lock on our elected legislators, and the body politic is further weakened by a recent wave of gold collar crime that shows no sign of abating. And why would it? These criminals have found a way to collar the gold and not get collared. They've figured out that the best way to stay on the right side of the law is to make sure they stay on the *writing* side of the law. After all, if you get to make the law, it saves you the trouble of breaking it.

Now still, there are some laws that cannot be broken. But they can be stretched. Yes, in this cover-your-ass world lawyers are indispensable, especially those who have mastered the art of using their energetic field — what the Chinese call "ch'i" (pronounced "chee") — to take unfair advantage. *Ch'i Ting* it is called. Thanks to this ancient practice, attorneys can now stretch the law to cover even the biggest ass! Of course, this costs plenty of money. If you think legal advice is expensive, you should see what they charge for *illegal* advice. And companies spend pretty freely, because guess who's ultimately picking up the tab?

Unfortunately, greedlock is contagious and can easily be spread in a toxic environment. Symptoms include a closed hand, a tight fist, and an over-exercised strong-arm. Unchecked, greedlock can paralyze the body politic, leaving it susceptible to those who believe only in the Law of Grabbity: That with a big enough hand and a strong enough arm, you can grab anyone's privates with impunity.

Newton discovers the Law of Grabbity.

Deficit Inattention Disorder

With our own government engaged in risky debt-defying stunts, it is no wonder that the consumers have developed Deficit Inattention Disorder. This condition — thought to be exacerbated by large doses of mass media — weakens the consumer's resistance with a barrage of advertising, while credit card companies feed on them to make sure they buy, buy, buy until it's bye-bye money. The credit card industry, meanwhile, doesn't take much interest in Deficit Attention Disorder sufferers until they max out their cards — then they take plenty of interest, up to 28%. Unchecked, Deficit Inattention Disorder can lead to actual fiscal paralysis and almost certain debt.

And while we are dealing with our own personal disorder caused by inattention to our deficit, we have become enablers for our government to do the same thing. After all, one of the most insidious symptoms of a Military Industrial Complex is getting drunk on power, and then going on a spending orgy buying any and every weapon on your wish list. And because so much money can be spent in secret, the military gets to go on this shopping spree unshoparoned.

Even though those who suffer from Deficit Inattention Disorder have plenty of material possessions, deep down they have an impoverished spirit. While some individuals may actually have a debt-wish, many of the near-debt experiences people suffer are self-generated, and so is the cure. In other words, when you come to a debt-end road, time to turn around!

Let's Get Down to the Real Needy-Greedy, Okay?

Here is the joke. We own nothing, really. There are no material possessions we can take out of here when we go. So it is definitely true that money can't buy happiness. But it can rent it for a while, and we humans are clearly renters. And ever since the first coin jingled against the second coin, we have been stuck in a dysfunctional dance trying to possess something we already have yet cannot really own.

So I say after all these millennia, it's time for us to get down to the real needy-greedy. This back and forth dance between need and greed is getting us nothing but bruised toes. The needy blame the greedy, and the greedy blame the needy. Whether your mantra is "Bleed the greedy and feed the needy!" or "Bleed the needy and feed the greedy!" it's the same song and dance, the same old needy-greedy.

But maybe we don't need to be needy *or* greedy. Maybe if we used the most abundant human resource on the planet — imagination — to multiply our less abundant natural resources, we could create our own loaves and fishes. Feeding two birds with one scone — that's what I call supply-side spirituality!

★ PROFILES IN ENCOURAGEMENT

Could Cradle-to-Cradle Be the Cradle of a Truly Civilized Civilization? William McDonough Thinks So

What if we decided to lift our heads up above the old needy-greedy, and look beyond those dueling dualities, capitalism and socialism? What if we gave up our low-class class warfare in favor of a high-class peace? Could we find a way to truly beat our swords into plowshares instead of into each other? Maybe the road not yet traveled is what William McDonough calls "ecologism."

We hear the argument all the time: "It's the economy, stupid!" "No, it's the ecology!" And what we're doing now seems to be helping neither. Maybe it's the *synergy,* an economy based on ecology, where — paradoxically — unlimited economic growth can take place within the natural laws of a thriving ecology. Now of course this sounds pretty utopian, but given where we seem to be headed, I figure it's worth a look, right?

William McDonough is a true American Evolutionary. An architect, visionary and designer, when he was teaching at the University of Virginia, he actually lived in a home designed by Thomas Jefferson. And just in time for the American Evolution, he is promoting an economy based on his updated version of "life, liberty and the pursuit of happiness": Ecological intelligence, justice and fun.

As an architect and corporate consultant, William McDonough can say things to corporate CEOs that the rest of us can only mutter under our breath. He keeps asking them one simple question over and over again: What do you do? And after all the usual answers come out — we make cars, we employ thousands, etc., etc. — he gets them to cop to the bottom bottom line: *We create toxic waste.* Just about every manufacturer does.

And then with the calm moral authority of a scientist, he tells them exactly what their toxic chemical residoodoo is doing. "The plastic heads on your dolls are poisoning little girls," he says, and tells them how and why. And he challenges them with another question: "Is harming children part of your design? It's not? Then it's a part of your de facto design, because it is what is happening, by design or otherwise." Then he challenges the company to focus their abundant imagination to see how those very same things can be made economically and ecologically.

McDonough talks the talk, and he walks the walk. His book, *Cradle to Cradle: Remaking the Way We Make Things,* feels a little different, a little heavier than most books its size. "This book is not a tree," he tells us. It's actually made from plastic resins and fillers, and is 100% recyclable. And waterproof too. Along with chemist Michael Braungart, he has founded a company McDonough Braungart Design Chemistry (MBDC) to help companies make environmentally safe products that are less wasteful and less expensive to make than traditionally manufactured products.

The "cradle to cradle" design protocol is "waste = food." In other words, waste is not an option. Whatever by-products are produced must be completely safe and reusable. MBDC's first design project was to develop a collection of compostable fabrics for Designtex, which manufactures commercial upholstery, wall coverings, office panel systems and window treatments. Out of the 8,000 prospective dyes and chemicals they could use, they found just 38 that qualified. Working with a small Swiss fabric mill, they developed a toxin-free fiber and a production process so clean, it produces potable water and scrap felt trimmings that local farmers can use to mulch their strawberry fields . . . forever.

McDonough designed the Herman Miller furniture facility in Zeeland, Michigan and the Gap corporate offices in San Bruno, California, both of which are models for human-friendly and earth-friendly facilities. The solar and geothermal-powered building he designed for Oberlin College in Ohio generates more energy than it uses. His latest ambitious project is to convert the Ford River Rouge plant in Michigan from an ugly, polluting behemoth to a producer of "clean" cars and non-toxic by-products.

William McDonough has confounded — and inspired — both regulation-wary businessfolks and organically-dyed-in-the-wool environmentalists by insisting we can have a healthy economy *and* a healthy ecology if we "consider nature as a model inventor, not an inconvenience to be evaded or controlled." Regulations, he says, "are a symptom of design failure." And indeed, he has motivated companies like Nike and Ford to create an earth-healthy production process that would make regulation redundant.

Growth is good, he says, provided what is grown is healthy, beautiful and functional. "We see a world of abundance, not limits," he says, "and with intelligent designs, bigger and better is possible in a way that replenishes, restores, and nourishes the rest of the world."

Now there's an encouraging concept. Along with the bottom line, there is a "top line": Science as applied spirituality, working in harmony with Earth for the greatest good of all. After all, what good are our greatest spiritual goods if they never make their way from the Good Book to the Good Life? It just may be that commerce is where the Spirit meets the road. Yes, Jesus saves. But we humans invest, and maybe it is our investments that hold the key to saving the planet. Maybe we need to go eight strong innings, and *then* bring Jesus in to pick up the save.

Five Ways to Feed Two Birds With One Scone

OK. By now we realize that we humans have been a big part of the problem, and now is the time for us to dissolve the problem in a solution. And here is the solution: We are the solution. Problem dissolved.

Actually, it sounds easier than it is. But with an ever-increasing supply of us humans, we are quickly becoming the most plentiful resource on the planet. So why not use us? If we are a resource, why shouldn't we be resourceful? Why not combine prayer and imagination and good old playful work, and supply solutions that will meet the demands of the new millennium?

Look at us. The Bible tells us to "be fruitful and multiply," and here we've been stuck in fruitless division. So what can we do to feed two (or more) birds with one scone and create both a healthy income and a healthy outcome? Here are some ideas.

1. Buy Products With Healthier By-Products
The big corporations vote with their dollars, so why not us? So the first step is to consciously and conscientiously support those companies that are delivering the goods, and withhold commerce from those delivering the bads. The Recourses and Resources section in the back of this book will offer some places to find out not just who's who, but what's what.

Support healing, beauty and functionality in all its forms. If we truly want to wage peace, let's support more of us making our wages peacefully. We often hear that war is a necessary evil, so let's invest in peace as a necessary good. Wealth is healthy, when there is a wealth of health. You know what a sign of a healthy culture is? Well-heeled healers. Let's spend our wealth so we become wealthier in health.

2. Put the Whole Country on Wealthfair
Want to know how to transform the needy-greedy for good? Put the whole country on a vigorous Wealthfair program. Imagine children from an early age — rich or poor, urban, rural or suburban — learning how to use their skills to provide needed services and be paid a fair price. After all, the best antidote for a deadly 'hood is livelihood. With plenty of talent and willingness, and

105

plenty that needs doing, there is more than enough for us all to become fairly wealthy, and wealthy fairly.

3. Go For Higher Interest Rates

If we want wealth to stretch out in all directions to all corners of society, well then, we must increase our Greenspan — and raise interest rates. With so many interesting things to do, too many people waste their precious time working at jobs they aren't really interested in. Low interest rates have been known to cause depression, not to mention ineffectiveness and inefficiency at work. On the other hand, high interest pays off. If you are highly interested in things that have true value, your interest will pay great dividends. Value what you appreciate, and it will appreciate in value.

4. Practice Fung Shun

You know, one thing the Republicans have right is, they really know how to get down to business. They don't spend a lot of time ruminating, reading "The Leisure of the Theory Class." They understand and practice Fung Shun, the ancient Chinese art of taking care of business. And they remind us that even though we would love to give a helping handout to everyone, helping isn't helpful when it makes people helpless. It's like the old proverb: Give a man a fish and he will eat for a day. But teach a man to fish, and he'll say, "To heck with work. I'm going fishing!"

Of course, we have to take care that our business is taking care of not just our immediate family, but all our relations. If we want to beat our swords into plowshares, we must all do our fair share of the plowing, and then plow our share back into increasing both fun and the function on the planet.

5. Put Those Conservatives to Work — Conserving!

In a world that has been spending precious nonrenewable resources far too liberally, we need every conservative we can get. After all, what better use for a true conservative than to help us conserve? Maybe we need a National Conservative Conservatory where conservatives could learn the pros of conserving, instead of merely serving the cons (particularly those neocons). I know this sounds radical, but what if we channeled conservatives into their natural calling of conservation? There could be an entirely new career path as they hired themselves out to companies as sufficiency experts.

May I Have This A Bun Dance With You?

So here is the bottom line. Abundance is ours to have, if we get up off of our bottoms, move our buns and start dancing. Time to stop sitting on your assets stuck in scare city. And listen, it's a lot more fun to face the music if we all face it together.

May I have this ABunDance with you?
Sun, earth, water and air
We're waltzing with life on this beautiful planet
With love there's so much we can share

Consider the birds and the trees
And the flowers that sing in the breeze
They don't need to hurry
They never worry
They love to do as they please

Seek and you will find
You gotta trust your sacred mind
You don't have to believe
Ask, and you will receive
You don't have to wait for a sign

There are no reasons for greed
The earth provides more than we need
It's just the human race
That keeps stuffing its face
At an ever-increasing speed

From "Drive Your Karma, Curb Your Dogma" CD. Music by Daniel Taylor, lyrics by Daniel Taylor and Steve Bhaerman.

SWAMI ANSWERS YOUR QUESTIONS, AND YOU WILL QUESTION HIS ANSWERS.

Who Needs Money, Anyway?

Dear Swami:

I've heard that the entire world money system is on the verge of collapse. Are you concerned about this too?

—Shakti Rich,
Kashpur, India

Dear Shakti:

Well, let us begin by asking, what is money, anyway? For some, it is a medium of exchange. For fortunate others with a fortune, it is a large of exchange. For far too many, it is a small that has just gotten two sizes smaller. But in truth, money is simply a representation of what we find valuable. Obviously, right now we must find conflict awfully valuable because we've certainly invested in it.

The first money was created so that people could easily exchange goods and services without having to carry around cows, goats, pigs and sheep in their pocket. Talk about fumbling for change. Sorry, I don't have change for a pig. And one chicken? You call that a tip?

And because ancient cattle owners didn't want to have a

cow trying to make a fair trade, money was invented. The first coins were precious stones, beads, shells, and later pounded metals. And after awhile, people began to amass large amounts of this "money" and had to find a place to stash it. Those who had no vault started looking for a storage unit, and the first bank was born. And look how far we've come. With the world economy even more usurer-friendly today, no-vault insurance is a high-premium business.

But back to your question. What if it all fell apart? Well, so what? Would there still be food growing and people who want to eat? Would we still need buildings built? And how about a massage every now and then? And a movie? We would figure out a way for the currents to flow, even if we had to make our own currency. And with our own currency, what do we need with theirs?

Currency is the lifeblood of the body politic, and in a healthy body politic money flows where love goes. After all, shouldn't the lifeblood be pumped by the heart? The needy-greedy struggle stops the flow. We are taught that commercial life is about diverting the currents of currency into exclusive pools. Why doesn't anyone ever suggest that we just do a rain dance together instead? Once we own up to not owning the world, and start owning our actions instead, we will see the ownus is on us. And we will invent any currency currently needed.

Is There a Reward in the NAFTA-Life?

Dear Swami:

When that NAFTA free trade bill was signed ten years ago, we were promised that free trade would mean prosperity for all. And yet here we are ten years later, and all of OUR jobs here in Mexico have been outsourced to China. Where is our reward? What's the real story on globalization?

—Juana Cruz,
Sueño de los Santos, Mexico

Dear Juana,

It is sad but true. How many people were promised riches in the NAFTA-life, yet never reaped their reward? Yes, the world is getting smaller every day (or is it we who are getting larger?) and free trade is the wave of the future. Just as sure as our jobs went south, yours are going east. But the good news is, what goes around comes around.

So it all depends on what kind of globalization we're talking about. Is it "gobble-ization" where a few fat turkeys gobble up everything? Is it — God forbid — "goebbelization" where we use impropaganda to make it look like the rape of the planet is consensual?

I say if we're going to globalize, might as well ask the globe. What would the Earth say? Probably something like this: "This is your planet speaking, welcome to Spaceship Earth. All passengers and crew are welcome, as long as they abide by the operating system called the Golden Rule. Love thy neighbor, and that includes all our relations."

How the globe shapes up is up to us. It all depends on whether we worship short-term profits or listen to Long-Term Prophets.

Should We Be Doing More With Less?

Dear Swami:

For years, environmentalists have been talking about doing more with less, and that seems right up my alley, considering I lost my job and my apartment, and just about all of my possessions have been repossessed. I now have nothing, and am virtually homeless. Any advice, Swami?

—Lucinda Street,
Brooklyn, New York

Dear Lucinda:

You've come to the right Swami. Not only have I been

doing more with less, I have been doing a whole lot with nothing. Seeing the success I've had with my Sound of Silence Meditation Tape, I've branched out into an entire line of products that cost nothing to make, use up no resources whatsoever, and are completely recyclable and renewable. Because of the proliferations of toxins in our environment, many people suffer from environmental allergies — like those who cannot stand to be around any kind of perfume. For their benefit I have come up with a completely odorless cologne! And I am marketing it under the brand name, Non-Scents.

But back to your situation. My advice is, begin by looking on the bright side. With no possessions, you have thrown off the yoke of consumerism. And having nothing, you can be completely worry-free because you have nothing to lose. You are free from car payments, insurance payments, and utility payments. With nothing to worry about, you are free to hire yourself out to the multitudes of others who are burdened with worries, and charge them each a modest fee to do their worrying for them. I mean, what do you care? It's not your worry, it's theirs. And with even just a few dollars a day from even a small portion of all the worried people in Brooklyn, you can make a pretty nice living as a mercenary worrier.

Does the Rat-Race Just Make Us a Race of Rats?

Dear Swami:

I've read my fill of news stories about corporations throwing their sizable weight around to stack the deck against the rest of us, and frankly I'm wondering when we're going to say, "We're mad as hell and we're not gonna take it anymore?" I say it's time we put these corporate rats in the appropriate cages!

—Orestes Matafakas,
Detroit, Michigan

Dear Orestes,

While I can understand how you can be enraged by this outrage, please remember that there relatively few gold collar criminals, and the rest of those you refer to as "rats" are just humans caught up in the rat race. In a way, all of us are stuck in some kind of maze looking for our share of the cheese. After all, haven't we all been trained to salivate at the sight of products as part of the all-consuming religion of consumption? Even if we ourselves haven't enlisted in the salivation army, let us have mercy on those poor rats trying to overtake others before someone undertakes them. So here is the good news. All rats are trainable! All we need to do within corporations (or anywhere else for that matter) is catch them in the act of doing something right and reward them.

And for the rest of us, maybe it's time to skip acquire practice and sing a different tune. Remember back in the 80s where they told you to invest in diamonds and store food? Well, here it is now and you realize we'd all be better off investing in hearts and giving food away. Happier and wiser, you realize it's not who dies with the most toys, it's whoever lives with the most joys that wins.

But Seriously, Folks . . .

We vote not just with our ballots, but with our pocketbooks and our checkbooks.

What if we as individuals, as communities, as a society invested our money, attention, time and resources only in what is truly healing and helpful?

What if we encouraged and empowered more people and communities to get up off of their assets, move their buns and dance together to make the commonwealth uncommonly wealthy?

Why, we could reap a world win!

Revitalize the Body Politic

How to Exercise Our Rights and Re-Constitute the Constitution

"Time to pump ironies and do free press presses"

W e don't need spin doctors to tell us that the body politic is in pretty bad shape. Electile dysfunction, truth decay, hardening of the artistries, loss of heart. And now the body politic is losing its voice as well, as many once-active cells are feeling like the Silenced Majority. Even mild-mannered Democrats have gotten so frustrated that they've been heard to mutter the F-word when talking about our current regime . . . you know, fascism.

The Not-See Menace

Indeed, Not-Seeism has become rampant. That is where, despite all of the evidence, there are those who insist on not seeing the truth. And the best way to deal with the Not-See menace is to shine enough light on the public sector that even the blind can see through the Irony Curtain. So let's shine the torch of liberty worldwide by shining the

The Not-See Salute

light of truth here, and by each becoming a healthy, active cell in the body politic. We need to exercise our rights, pump ironies and do free press presses in order to build the political muscle to counteract a regime that's been on steroids for years.

Let's Turn Devotees Into Votees

So let's begin by exercising our basic rights, shall we? First of all, we must exercise our right to vote. Those of you who decided years ago that politics was too dirty for an angelic spiritual being like yourself, time to get over that. Swami's mission is to turn every devotee into a . . . votee. And let's support those busy moms who don't vote because they don't have child-care, by offering rides and babysitting so they can vote for a more child-caring world. Remember that we vote each and every minute with our attention, so let's put our attention on love, life and laughter instead of fear. Fear is the toxic conditioning behind the current toxic conditions.

Pump Ironies to Strengthen the Body Politic

Wanna build muscle? Nothing like pumping ironies. You know those huge ironies that we end up swallowing whole — like, for example, the Holy Land being one of the most violent places on earth? Time to bring these into consciousness, and use them as irony supplements to strengthen the body politic. The Irony Curtain is built of unacknowledged ironies. Dissolve those ironies in a warm solution of laughter, and the light will shine through. Here are a few undigested ironies to chew on:

√ The Land of the Free has more people behind bars per capita than any other nation in the "free world."

√ We have a commander-in-chief who, when it was his turn to serve, didn't even bother finishing the light duty he was privileged to get to avoid the heavy duty duty.

√ We've incarcerated, brutalized and humiliated thousands of innocent Iraqis in the name of giving them freedom.

√ To keep the promise of "no child left behind," our Misleader has set the country back 20 years so we fall back to where that last poor kid is.

√ We consume 30% of the world's resources, then spend millions trying to lose weight.

With heavy, undigested ironies like these weighing us down, no wonder we find ourselves gaining weightiness.

Do Free Press Presses

If Will Rogers were alive today, he'd be saying, "All I know is what I *don't* read in the papers." If we want to restore integrity to government so that lie-ability is no longer an asset, we must press the press to tell the truth. We recommend doing phone-ups and free press presses at least three times a week. Call your local newspaper editor and TV stations and ask them to uncover the cover-ups. Email stories from truthout.com, and ask them to put it on the front page. If you get your truthful news online, support these sources financially — put your money where your mouse is!

With Two Strong Wings, We Can Reap a World Win

A balanced body politic needs two strong wings to fly right. Right now, we have one very strong right wing — and we are flying wrong. But just because the Right is wrong, that doesn't make the Left right. The eagle needs the wisdom of both wings to soar. That's why we need more forums, and fewer againstums. In each community, folks from all across the political spectrum need to get together and see what they're all "for." Imagine, all sides working together for the common good, weaving a web of mass construction to make the commonwealth uncommonly wealthy.

I'm not so sure about this, Orville!

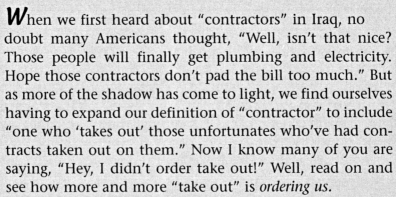

Soldiers of Misfortune and the World's Missing Fortune

When we first heard about "contractors" in Iraq, no doubt many Americans thought, "Well, isn't that nice? Those people will finally get plumbing and electricity. Hope those contractors don't pad the bill too much." But as more of the shadow has come to light, we find ourselves having to expand our definition of "contractor" to include "one who 'takes out' those unfortunates who've had contracts taken out on them." Now I know many of you are saying, "Hey, I didn't order take out!" Well, read on and see how more and more "take out" is *ordering us*.

Yes, contractor sounds more civil and civilian than "mercenary." But the truth is, Private Military Firms are mercenary indeed — to the tune of a $100 billion a year.

The hired guns of this brave new century are way more than hired guns. They're hired intelligence, hired helicopters, hired jets. And they will apparently lower themselves to do anything they are hired to do.

In Iraq, one of every ten "soldiers" (about 20,000) is a private employee, up from one in a hundred during the Gulf War. The key phrase is "plausible deniability" which translated into English means, "You better not tell me what you are doing." So it's not just gays in the military being told, "don't ask, and don't tell." Anything that needs to be done that we don't want to know about, who better to do it than someone who we've asked not to tell us? With lack of oversight and yet plenty of overlooking, is it any wonder that human rights have been superceded by inhuman rites?

Now while all of the huge Private Military Firms play like legitimate corporations (or even legitimate subsidiaries of legitimate corporations), the fact is you don't have to scratch too deeply to find folks who've been ordering "take out" since the 70s. For example, Hod Hahanit, staffed by former Israeli army officers, was involved in the assassination of two Colombian presidential candidates and the bombing of an airliner.

Then there's the South African 32nd Reconnaissance Battalion who didn't let the end of apartheid keep them apart. And the Soviet Alphas who formed a private company after the fall of the Soviet Union. Estimates are that 70% of former KGB are still working for somebody somewhere. And if the KGB is serving take out, it ain't at KFC.

A little closer to home — way too close to home, if you ask me — we have Halliburton, specifically Kellogg Brown & Root, Halliburton's subsidiary. Now if you think your contractor padded the bill, check this out:

√ During the Balkan Wars, KB&R failed to deliver or "severely overcharged" the U.S. Army on four out of seven of it's obligations.

✓ A subsequent Government Accounting Office report indicated that KB&R was still on the payroll with "contract employees sitting idly most of the time." (Looking on the bright side, in this case, idle hands *don't* do the devil's work.)

✓ Pentagon officials were able to lop off $72 million from the contract when they realized they were being overcharged for unneeded power generation equipment.

✓ In 2002, KB&R paid $2 million to settle a suit with the Justice Department alleging the company had defrauded the government in the dismantling of California's Fort Ord.

✓ During the first Bush Administration, then Secretary of Defense Dick Cheney hired KB&R to privatize some "routine army functions." A few years later, Cheney became CEO of Halliburton. (I know you coincidence theorists are going to have a field day with this one.)

✓ As CEO of Halliburton, he helped KB&R land a $2.2 billion contract in the Balkans. (Wait a minute. This many coincidences can't be merely coincidental. This must be *synchronicity!*)

Another contractor in Iraq is DynCorp (in Colombia they call it "dyin' core"), another first-ballot shoo-in for the Hall of Shame:

✓ Multinational Monitor voted them one of the 10 worst companies of 2002, and considering the stiff competition, that is quite a dishonor.

✓ They were subjected to a lawsuit by Ecuadorian citizens who were poisoned by the defoliant spray they used to eradicate the coca crop in Colombia. While they didn't manage to eradicate the coca crop, they did manage to make 1,100 people sick.

✓ In Bosnia, DynCorp employees were allegedly involved with the underage sex slave trade. The whistleblowers were fired, and the perpetrators never faced charges.

✓ DynCorp's former chairman and current board member is Herbert Winokur, who was until recently chairman of the Enron Finance Committee. Supposedly, he had oversight over what ended up being Enron's financial dealings, but he claimed ignorance. Hmm. Must have been an oversight.

So, is this the hooded face of warfare for the new century? Peter W. Singer, in his staid and sober thesis on Corporate Warriors, matter-of-factly compares the current state of affairs to "a return to the dynamics of 16th Century Europe where wealth and military capability went hand-in-hand." And speaking about "affairs," a quick look at who's sleeping with who offers a sobering picture of what's what:

✓ Blackwater (hmm . . . makes you long for Whitewater, eh?), the firm whose "contractors" were killed at Fallujah, has hired the Alexander Strategy Group to lobby Congress on regulating private military firms in Iraq. Interestingly, Alexander's chairman Ed Buckham was former chief of staff to House Majority Leader Tom DeLay (R-Texas).

✓ Another contractor, CACI, hired the Livingston Group to provide the same services for them. The Livingston in the group is former House Appropriations Chairman Bob Livingston (R-Louisiana). Livingston was heir-apparent to Newt Gingrich as House Speaker until he tripped over his you-know-what during the Clinton impeachment hearings. When he was outed for his own sexual transgressions, he was forced to retire to "private life," where presumably the life of his privates will come under less scrutiny.

✓ Titan, another important contractor, has spent $1.29 million since 2000 to lobby in Washington. Among Titan's titans is Michael Herson, who was special assistant to Dick Cheney when Cheney was Secretary of Defense. Titan's political action committee, by the way, has contributed 12 times as much to Republicans than to Democrats.

So there we have it, folks. In case you were wondering where our commonwealth has gone, it has gone into private pockets of influence that are deep enough to fund their own private armies. Those doddering structures called "nation states" are becoming little more than formalities in the gobble-ized and unfortunately, goebbelized global economy.

So what's the good news? The good news is, now you know. You can no longer plead ignorance as one of the "innocent" Not-Sees who failed to see what's been obvious to just about everyone but us. Once we see what has been turning our democracy into a mockracy, we can diagnose the disease in the body politic — and help find the cure.

But Seriously, Folks . . .
Can We Say the F-Word?

The F-word. Nobody really wants to say it out loud, particularly not in polite company. But with the body politic as compromised as it is, maybe it's time we utter the unutterable: Fascism. A loathsome disease, a cancer of the body politic, an abnormal growth where all the tissue turns to muscle, and the heart is squeezed like a lemon. Ugh. I know we don't even want to think about it, but the good news is, it's completely curable in its early stages.

So that is why we recommend a regular self-examination for the body politic. So let's do this keeping-abreast exam together, okay? Now the following list of symptoms of fascism are merely precursors, and if we address these imbalances pronto, we may very well avoid the actual curse of the affliction itself.

Know the Fourteen Danger Signs of Fascism! The Laugh You Save May Be Your Own

Take this simple test. First, answer the questions. Then, question the answers. The laugh you save may be your own.

1. Nationalism.

✓ Have you been exposed to excessive nationalism radiating from the mass media? Have you noticed any abnormal swelling of pride?

✓ Have you seen more photo ops featuring flag-draped politicians than photo ops featuring flag-draped coffins?

2. Disdain for Human Rights.

✓ Have you recently become aware of human rights being violated by inhuman wrongs?

✓ Are we being told that our enemies are "inhuman" so we can dehumanize them — and not have to treat them humanely?

3. Identification of Enemies/Scapegoats as a Unifying Cause.

✓ Have you noticed more demagogues pointing a finger at some villainous "dem" as a danger to "us"?

✓ Dem terrorists? Dem Iraqis? Dem Democrats?

4. Supremacy of the Military.

✓ Are schools being inundated with zillions of dollars in secret funding — and the Defense Department having to raise money through bake sales? (Gotcha. Just checking to see if you were paying attention.)

5. Rampant Sexism.

✓ Do we have an Administration that will tell a woman what she can or cannot do with her unborn fetus, but will think nothing of offing 10,000 fully-born Iraqi civilians?

✓ Is our government suffering a famine of the feminine? Did we miss it, or did George Bush urge Congress to pass the Matriot Act after 9/11 to help turn worldwide sympathy into worldwide healing and forgiveness?

6. Controlled Mass Media.

✓ Have you seen an increase in cases of Depressed Press Syndrome, an auto-immune response where the press suppresses itself?

✓ Did you know that the President bought each member of the White House Press Corps their own pair of knee-pads?

7. Obsession with National Security.
✓ Have you noticed the insecurities market going through the roof?
✓ Are you beginning to feel the need to be protected from those being paid to protect you?

8. Religion and Government are Intertwined.
✓ Have you noticed a sharp increase in selfish-righteousness, where righteousness masks selfishness?
✓ Do you see zealots on fire to put the Ten Commandments up at our courthouses, but not the Golden Rule?

9. Corporate Power is Protected.
✓ Has private excess replaced public access?
✓ Do you suspect the government and business are snuggled in bed together performing unspeakable acts, but you don't know for sure because they're hiding behind the Irony Curtain?

10. Labor is Suppressed.
✓ Have you noticed a proliferation of those MallWart stores where the workers can't even afford the low prices?
✓ Do we have too few employed, too many deployed?

11. Disdain for Intellectuals and the Arts.
✓ Have you observed an increase in assaholism, characterized by arrogant ignorance?
✓ Have you noticed more ignoranuses in positions of power? (Remember, you are under oaf.)

12. Obsession with Crime and Punishment.
✓ Have you noticed an increase in covert ops? Overt cops?
✓ Have you noticed a sharp increase in prison construction, a growing incarcenoma on the body politic?

13. Rampant Cronyism and Corruption.

✓ Have you been a victim of gold collar crime in the past year? Have your life savings evaporated into "past life savings?"

✓ Are you beginning to get the impression we're being hoodwinked by a bunch of hoods winking at each other's transgressions?

14. Fraudulent Elections.

✓ Have you come to realize that the only paper trail in our electoral system is the one we accidentally track in from the bathroom?

✓ Is the body politic being leveraged to "stay the course" because these are "dangerous times" (you know, don't change horse's asses in the middle of an extreme)?

Adapted from an article entitled "Fascism Anyone?" by Laurence W. Britt . . . Council on Secular Humanism, Spring, 2003 - Volume 23, No. 2

★ PROFILES IN ENCOURAGEMENT

Bringing Down a Dictator

*I*t was 1998. Serbian President Slobodon Milosevic had begun his "ethnic cleansing" campaign against the Albanians. Albanians were uprooted from their homes, put in concentration camps, killed if they resisted — and sometimes even when they didn't. In response, the United States began a bombing campaign against Serbia.

In the midst of this dark time, a small group of young Serbians — most of them between 18 and 20 — began to ask an unasked question: "What's wrong with this picture?" There was something about killing and being bombed in return that wasn't . . . well, it wasn't life-affirming. They realized this didn't represent the future they wanted to live in, and they decided to do something about it. Within two years, this movement that started with a few courageous kids and a xerox machine had brought down one of the most brutal dictators in the world. There's a video, **Bringing Down a Dictator** (which you can buy or rent) that tells the inspiring story of how imagination, playfulness and nonviolence helped awaken the body politic, and created the political will to topple a despot.

He's Finished!

These young people began with an outrageous premise: Slobodon Milosevic's regime stood for death and repression instead of life and growth, and on that basis alone had no legitimacy. Early on, they came up with a slogan that they painted and plastered everywhere: "He's Finished." They dropped leaflets from buildings, they engaged in clever public actions, and they caught the attention of the U.S. State Department, who helped fund their communications — including funny TV commercials. In one, a woman is about to wash a shirt that has a picture of Slobodon on the front. She touts the campaign as the only effective way to "get out the dirt," pulls the shirt out of the wash, and voilå — the picture of Slobodon is gone.

Within eighteen months this small group of young people managed to get a gaggle of quarreling political parties to choose one opposition candidate to support. (Are you listening, Ralph Nader?) At this point, the Milosevic government began feeling the heat, and so they arrested some of the movement's leaders. Large groups of young people gathered by the prison with amplified megaphones instructing the jailers not to harm their friends. In all of this, there was never a confrontation with police or military. Movement leaders always made it clear that the young people who were in military or police uniforms were not the enemy.

Hey, We're All <u>Us</u>!

With worldwide focus on the election — there were American and UN observers to make sure votes were counted fairly — the opposition candidate was the clear winner. But Milosevic didn't see it that way. There was no "definitive winner," he declared, and there had to be a run-off. There followed a general strike, and hundreds of thousands of vehicles began making their way to the capitol, Belgrade. There were tense moments, but ultimately the young people in the military and police saw that the hundreds of thousands of people marching on the capitol were their brothers, sisters, aunts, uncles, nieces and nephews, parents and grandparents. Instead of being leveraged into "us vs. them," they realized "We're all US!" The military stepped aside, the palace was unguarded, and Milosevic fell.

Americans Need to Be More Hawkish!

Yes, it is understandable that peace-loving people would naturally be more dovish, hoping to dovetail their position with that of the hawks. But sometimes the best way to keep the peace is to keep a sharp, hawkish eye out. And to squawk when necessary.

Just try and take this from me!

For example, the Patriot Act. We need to be hawkish enough to point out that the Patriot "Act" is just an act to activate mindless patriotism, and de-activate mindful patriots who are actively asking questions. So we must watch our servants like hawks to make sure they

128

don't take liberties with our liberties — or steal our silver — to serve their own purpose.

And let's be hawkish in protecting our beloved Mom, Earth, from which all good things, like apple pie, grow. If you don't want a green, thriving vibrant planet, why don't you just go back to wherever you came from? Earth — love it or leave it.

Oh, and let's be hawkish in making sure that death-trip apocalyptic cults disguised as religions don't pull the world down their dead-end rat-hole.

Let's be hawkeyed in safeguarding the true economy — our world's commonwealth — and actively support that which makes us uncommonly wealthy by bringing value to the world. Let's be hawkish in the real pro-life movement, and support only what is life-giving. That way every born feed us will be given a better life.

We think doves are great, and we love to hear them coo. But when the coo-coo are cooking a coup, only a squawking hawk can protect us. Otherwise we're all dead pigeons.

How to Build a Strong Body Politic 12 Ways.

1. Repeal the Bill of Wrongs. Benjamin Franklin — who unlike the current White House occupant put his behind on the line for liberty — said, "Whoever would trade liberty for security deserves neither." With the so-called Patriot Act, those in power secure their security at the price of our liberty. Since the current Administration seems to be more terrified by the truth than anything else, any truth-teller runs the risk of being labeled a terrorist. Time for real patriots to bring down the Irony Curtain on this Patriot "Act."

2. Reform the Incontinental Congress. The parallels between now and the early days of our republic are striking. Before the Constitution was constituted, we had the Continental Congress. And now that the Constitution is being de-constituted, we have the Incontinental Congress pissing away our Constitutional rights by being an enabler for an Administration perpetrating unconstitutional wrongs. And pissing away our commonwealth to privatizing privateers who are paying top dollar to influence Congress so they can pay bottom dollar for use of public resources.

Here is how the Green Party can actually do something useful. Even though they don't have the funds to fluff up legislators, they can still give out Green Stamps each time they catch a legislator doing something right. At election time, these Green stamps are redeemable for Green Party support. That way we can give the green light to those who'll help us keep more of the "green" by growing local economies.

3. Pass the Transparency Amendment. To truly have representative government, we need to have transparency. Instead we have an apparent trance where citizens don't seem to mind that trillions of our taxpayer dollars seem to have vanished. Think about it. Somebody robs a 7/11 and the local media is johnny-on-the-spot. Someone comes forward with new evidence on 9/11 and no one wants to touch it.

But don't you think if you're being screwed, it's only fair to have a peek under the covers? Besides, if the body politic is going into recovery, the first step is to uncover what has been covered up. We need a Transparency Amendment to give we the people the power to strip search the government if we suspect our civil servants of being uncivil serpents. The body politic lost its election before it was satisfied back in 2000, and it won't happen again. Seeing the government naked is an absolute turn-on for the body politic, and that alone will help us sustain a healthy election for a change.

4. Celebrate Shadow Holidays. When we celebrate the shadow, the shadow gets overshadowed by light and laughter, and we are actually able to learn from our mistakes! We've already mentioned ManHog Day, where we are once again reminded that unless we see our own shadow, we face a long season in the darkness.

Then there's Columbo's Day, honoring the great detective, where we the people get to poke around and ask curious questions: "Now . . . let me get this straight. A trillion dollars just disappeared from the treasury . . . and we're wondering how we're gonna pay our national debt? I'm not clear on this. Honey, I misplaced a trillion dollars. Tell the kids it's coming out of their allowance."

We Americans are known for generosity, and one of the things we've been most generous with is providing weaponry to other countries to help them keep their upheavals down. Repressing upheavals is full-time work, and that's the business we're in. So let us give tanks. And guns. And jets. Let's celebrate Tanksgiving each year, and reflect on how much money it is costing to keep people suppressed when it would be lot cheaper and more fun to help them go free. And as we sit ready to devour our holiday turkey, pause for a moment to reflect on the overstuffed turkeys who've been having a holiday devouring our resources.

5. Establish the Anti-Defecation League and the Canary Project. With assaholism rampant at the highest echelons of power, and a bully attitude of "You're either with us or against us," people with unpopular beliefs — or even believed to have unpopular beliefs — could very easily find themselves on a shit-list. Yes, in these suspicious times when any interesting person can become a person of interest, we need the Anti-Defecation League to protect innocent non-terrorists from chickenshit, horse shit, bullshit — and most dangerous of all — elephant shit. In fact, I see them providing bullshit-proof vests to any reporters going into the electoral war zone.

SPOTTED OWL   BLUE BUTTERFLY   WHISTLE BLOWER

ENDANGERED SPECIES

And let's immediately expand the Endangered Species Act to protect truth-tellers. What with all of the ongoing ethic cleansing the Administration is doing, truth-tellers are becoming all too rare. If the body politic is to make it through recovery, we must face the truth, and in order to face the truth, we gotta know the truth. So let's disabuse ourselves of any illusions, and make sure that those who point out abuses don't get abused themselves.

That is why we need the Canary Project to make sure our canaries can sing freely without getting snuffed. Just like in those mining days, if the canaries go, guess who's next? After all, no man is a canary island. And never misunderestimate the power of a canary's song to upset the set-up. In other words, you may look like the cat that swallowed the canary now, but just wait until some canary lets the cat out of the bag.

6. Freely Press the Press. Imagine if the most important part of your brain was purposely giving you inaccurate or incomplete information. Wouldn't you be pissed? Well, information is the nervous system of our democracy . . . and frankly, I'm pretty nervous about the system. Disney? I guarantee you Walt is crying in his cryogenic crypt. CBS — well, their name says it all. And Fox? When it comes to truth-telling they stop at nothing. Interestingly, as you numerologists know, the number for F-O-X is 6-6-6. So if you had them pegged as a marked beast, you're probably right.

Clearly the press is being pressed into service as part of the impropaganda machine, and we the people have to start doing free press presses. I say we can create the crosscurrents we choose by plugging and unplugging.

Imagine if 50 million Americans who want to feed the wolf of love unplugged from the unfree press for just one month. Imagine 50 million people calling their radio and TV stations, their newspapers and news magazines to tell them why they unplugged and what might bring them back into the fold.

And then what if we took our spending power and plugged it in to the alter native media not afraid to tell the truth and alter the natives for the better? Then, what if we shared what we were learning with an audience that's already listening? Radio listeners. Listen — radio listeners are listening! What if 50 million people appointed themselves to call Rush or Michael Savage or any of the other wrong-wing bully-shit artists out there, and began speaking freely? Plug the truth, and if they won't let you do that, unplug their phoney system by plugging it up with calls for the truth.

7. Put the Vice President in Charge of Vice. Why should Vice Presidents be traipsing around in undisclosed locations when they could be doing something truly useful? In this recovery program of honoring the shadow, we'd be fools not profit from the shadow as well. So I say, put the Vice President in charge of vice. Have him fly to meet with the Organization of Drug Producing Countries (DOPEC), and get us ALL a piece of the action. Instead of waging war against sin, why not share the wages?

Now this may sound a bit perverse to you, so I will relate a Zen Cohen my guru Harry Cohen Baba once told: In a little Texas town around the turn of the last century, the local madam came to the minister and said, "Reverend, I'd like to make amends for my life, and I want to donate everything I have to your church."

The minister said, "I need to think about that, ma'am. Could you come back tomorrow?"

She returned the next day and the minister had made up his mind. "I'm sorry, ma'am. I can't accept your offer."

She left, and one of the church people approached the minister. "Reverend, we need a new building. Why did you turn down her generous offer?"

"Because," the minister proclaimed, "her money is tainted money."

The man looked at the minister and said, "What do you mean, her money? It's OUR money!"

8. Clean Up the Sue-widge by Training Ombuddhasmen Instead.
No doubt about it. Sue-widge is clogging up our system, as we've turned more and more of our problems over to lawyers. And we've spent so much energy taking sides, that we forget that it's not the sides that give us the solution, it's the angles. So we need mediators to help all sides explore all angles.

That's why we need to train more "ombuddhasmen" (and, it goes without saying even though I'm saying it, "ombuddhaswomen") to help bring the Buddha nature to any situation to "make all beings happy." The ombuddhasman is trained to hear grievances, and help resolve them before they come to grief. Imagine how many full-blown flare-ups we could prevent, especially around those human fault lines.

9. Present the NO BULL PRIZE for Truth Telling. Time to speak the truth out loud, and encourage everyone else to joyfully and courageously do the same. Sure, we've made great strides in consciousness but if you can't break the soundless barrier, your new paradigms ain't worth four nickels.

If we're going to overcome cattlepsy, we must reward those who've been battling Mad Cowboy Disease and haven't gotten thrown by the bull. An inspiring example is Michael Moore, a sacred cowpoke if there ever was one. Last year, the Right to Laugh Party proudly presented the No Bull Prize to Sen. Robert Byrd (D-West Virginia) for speaking out in Congress about the incongruous policy of making peace in the Middle East by going to war. The inscription read, *"A Byrd in the hand is worth all the Bushes you got."*

10. Appoint a Supreme Court Jester. With so little to laugh about recently, we must make sure that laughter is supreme. A Supreme Court Jester will use laughter to restore equilibrium, and goodness knows all sides could use more Librium. The Jester is there to make sure that our leaders are fooly-realized, and realize their own foolishness before they go out and do something even more foolish.

I say, put a jester in every court so we always remember to put laughter before judgment, and unabashedly promote the FUNdamentalist credo of "All for fun, and fun for all." I see the jesters meting out cool and unusual punishment, sentencing wrongdoers to doing something right for a change, something positive and useful that benefits whole community.

11. Form CityZen Unions to Hold Forums Instead of Againstums. Every city, town and neighborhood needs to form its own CityZen Union, to meditate peacefully together and hold regular "forums" where citizens from all viewpoints come together and create solutions that none of them could have come up with on their own. This focusing on what we're "for" instead of what we're against will strengthen the body politic on the cellular level instead of getting cells adrenalized over imaginary threats. We need to come front and center to capture the heart of both parties and lead from the middle of the road, the middle of a new road that's wide enough to accommodate all who want to walk together.

12. Play Lead the Leader. No great leader to follow? No problem. Time for us to lead ourselves out of the bewilderness, and have our leaders follow us for a change. Let's form a "light" government to shadow the shadow government, a Pro-Visional Evolutionary NonGovernment that promotes an evolutionary vision without coercion . . . liberty and justice for all. Hey, whether we're soccer moms, NASCAR dads, or dykes on bikes, we all have this in common: We want our children to grow up in a more just, happy and healthy world. If we want our misleaders to step down, we must step up.

SWAMI ANSWERS YOUR QUESTIONS . . .
AND YOU WILL QUESTION HIS ANSWERS.

"I Blame the Psychics," Swami Says

Dear Swami:

You obviously have loads of wisdom and insight, so I'll ask you the key question: Who is really to blame for 9/11? And in the light of such a serious attack, is a military response justified?

—Xavier Onassis,
Kalispell, Montana

Dear Xavier:

I know this may sound hard to take, but I must be honest. I blame the psychics for 9/11. Think about it. All of those world famous psychics make their predictions in the National Enquirer each year, and not one of them ever comes true. So if only a psychic had predicted the 9/11 attack, it never would have happened. Never mind why didn't the Pentagon know? Why didn't the *psychics* know? At least they could have asked Jordan, Israel, Spain, and the Soviet Union. They all knew about it. The only ones who didn't know were the American people. And the psychics.

I must say, I've had to reconsider my own security considerations. Up until now, I've employed psychics at the door working as mental-detectors. Now I'm thinking about going with the clowns from the Secret Circus.

Anyway, in answer to your second question, it is important to look at the body politic as a whole and see that a disease of the body politic is always the result of an imbalance. Toxic human conditions caused by toxic human conditioning can often release free radicals into the mainstream, and we know what kind of damage they can do. And sometimes we do have to send in those Mr. T cells to dissolve toxic pockets. However, if we leave the terrain more toxic than we found it, the disease will return with a vengeance.

The problem with knee-jerk reactions is you generally end up kneeing the wrong jerk. And it starts to look like that Laurel and Hardy movie where the two of them get into a fight with another motorist and they end up destroying each other's cars. In fact, I had a dream the other night that George Bush was Stan Laurel and the body politic was played by Oliver Hardy. Ollie was berating Stan, "NOW look what you've done! Here's another fine Mesopotamia you've gotten us into!"

To me the message of this dream is clear: The body politic rested on its laurels, and the result was a foolhardy venture.

A RINO's Nose Out of Joint?

Dear Swami:

I'm one of those RINOs you hear about — Republican In Name

Only — who voted for George Bush last time because of his compassionate conservative stand. This time, though, I'm beginning to have my doubts. In the past, the Right has always felt a little more right to me, but what with the war, the lying, and the stonewalling of all opposition, I'm not sure. Any insights, Swami?

—Albie Yamunky-Zunkel,
Phoenix, Arizona

Dear Albie:

It is understandable that you have misgivings — or, in the President's case, mister-givings. After all, if a crash is imminent and the only way to avert disaster is a sharp turn to the left, to continue going right would be wrong. You're not alone. I see a lot of RINOs making themselves over for this election, and I predict that RINO-plasty will change the face of American politics.

The Lesser of Two Weasels

Dear Swami:

I'm tired of having to choose the lesser of two weasels every election day! And it's frustrating to me that the unthinking masses don't seem to know what's good for them. It has me so irked that just to make a statement I'm going to vote for some third party candidate. When will the body politic get smart?

—Russell Papers,
Newton, Massachusetts

Dear Russell:

Well, if you're talking about the old TV show "Get Smart," I would say the body politic is there right now. Over the past few years, the body politic has sounded a lot like Maxwell Smart: "Don't tell me we're in trouble." *"We're in trouble."* "I *told* you not to tell me that!" And I know that under such conditions, it is very easy to get so frustrated that you begin referring to "the masses" as "them asses."

However, those of us who have seen through the scam and think we're so smart must not give in to smartyrdom. Smartyrdom is a "smarter-than-thou" attitude guaranteed to lose friends and irritate people. It's just another form of selfish-righteousness that keeps us isolated and ineffective. It's how the Left got left, and consequently how the Right got right.

If you read the party charter carefully, you'll see that the Democratic Party has invited everyone. So why be a party-pooper? Don't stay home commiserating with a few close friends who agree with you. Come to the big party, and bring all the love, wisdom, smarts and votes you have. Come as a party-planner, not a party-crasher and help decide what gets served. Come to have fun, and remember the de-Texas two-step:

Step 1. De-Elect the Misleader.
Step 2. Lead the Newly Elected Leader.

And remember what Confucius probably said: "Those who fail to choose the lesser of two evils will end up with . . . the greater evil."

But Seriously, Folks . . .

Power corrupts, and absolute power corrupts absolutely. They say secrecy protects all of us, but mainly secrecy protects those who have something to hide.

So . . . do you believe we have to be international bullies and gangsters to thrive in the new century? Is this what our legacy is — making the world a bitter place? Or do we deserve a government we can trust that stands by example as a beacon for democracy?

Time to become proactionaries, and earn our own No Bull Prize.

Don't Get Even, Get Odd!

Politics As Unusual

*"Forget about getting even. If the Law of Karma is right,
odds are it will all even out in the end anyway."*

Yes, these are indeed serious times we live in, and the world is facing some serious problems — most of them caused by serious foolishness. Albert Einstein said that a problem cannot be solved at the level it was created, so maybe serious problems have humorous solutions. For levity can help us rise to the occasion and see the situation from a higher perspective. Gravity only brings us down.

Chain of Foolishness

A look at history reveals a chain, chain, chain of foolishness dating back to the first dysfunction at the junction. Cain slew Abel. Over what? A guy preaches love thy neighbor, so they hang him on a cross. What's so smart about that? And those of you who think that sage burning is a new age Native American practice should have been around during the dark ages, when they burned sages as a ritual to keep everyone else in line. And it persists today, as tremors and flare-ups continue along every human fault line on the planet.

In Odd We Trust

So how do we break this chain of foolishness? Well, first thing is to laugh heartily at the foolish habit we have of getting even — and start getting odd instead. An eye for an eye guarantees continued blindness. On the odder hand, every positive change or great innovation has come from some odd individual with a wild, crazy and laughable idea. Humans flying like birds . . . HA! An end to slavery . . . HA! Women voting . . . HA! An upstart start-up nation insisting on inalienable rights . . . HA! Guaranteed, when humor-ologists go back far enough in history to find the first laugh, it was probably at the oddball nutcase who invented the wheel.

A Just War is Still . . . Just War

Meanwhile, we accept the most blatant insanity as sane and normal. Like war. Think of how many years the U.S. stayed in Vietnam to "save face." I guess it takes an oddball to point out that war isn't face-saving, it's ass-losing. We stayed there to save face, and we ended up losing our ass instead. Take a look at the faces of those in charge. Would you lose your ass to save their face? And forget the idea of a "just war." Every war is justified as just . . . and that's what we've been left with: Just war.

Here's An Odd Idea: Let's Declare CODE GREEN

In the wake of the 9/11 attacks, Americans have been terrorized not just by terrorism, but by the war on terrorism. Our Department of Homeland Insecurity has even color-coded danger, to make sure we "see red" when they need us to. All this code-dependence has made most Americans sad and scared. But after all, these frightening colors are just a pigment of our imagination anyway, so why don't we try something odd and imagine something different? Imagine the yellow of fear and blue of the blues being dissolved in a warm solution of love, and blending into a healing green. Instead of fomenting anger and an emergency mentality, why not foment love and creativity and an emerge 'n see mentality instead? Time to emerge from the habit of getting even and see the odd solution that is just ridiculous enough to work! Let's declare Code Green!"

One Plus One = ONE

Here's another odd idea: To transform the fear and sadness associated with 9/11, let's declare January 11th as a worldwide day of affirming that we're all in this together . . . and celebrate 1/11. I'm one, you're one, and together We are One. Remember E Pluribus Unum? Each of us has been given a special gift — just for entering. You already are a winner! Code Green is an invitation to use your unique gift to do what has not yet been done . . . to weave yourself into a web of mass construction, so we all reap a world win.

★ TRULY UNBELIEVABLE

Getting Even — What an Odd Habit!

*W*e have a world at odds trying to get even.

We have suicide bombers and terrorists literally going ballistic.

We have our own forces unable to control the situation by the use of force, and left with the only thing left in their arsenal they know how to use — more force.

According to the aptly-named book, *Addicted to War,* since 1948 the U.S. has spent $15 trillion (for those who want to zero in on what that looks like, that's $15,000,000,000,000) on the military, which is "more than the value of all the factories, machinery, roads, bridges, water and sewage systems, airports, railroads, power plants, office buildings, shopping centers, schools, hospitals, hotels, houses, etc. in this country put together."

That's a lot of assets on the line. To those of us too

crazy to buy into the insanity that passes for sanity these days, that much ass on the line is asinine. And besides, as the world's greatest — or how about only — superpower, whom are we looking to get even with? Well, oddly enough, when you've used deadly force to become Number One, everyone treats you like number two. As the underdeveloped world looks to get even, so we're looking to stay ahead by going one up.

It all goes back to the feudal feuds, where we got into the habit of getting even. Even if you start out even, one goes one up, and then up goes the other in one-upsmanship, and it goes one up, and one up, and one up, and finally it's, "Oh yeah? Well, one-up yours!"

If only we had understood the Greeks. When they designed their first Olympic "competition" that word meant something different than it does today. According to William McDonough, "competition" originally meant, "to strive together." All of us racers in the human race, we've been mis-taught that competition means erasing other racers, and winning at all costs. Actually, we're all in this human race together, each of us striving to make our own best time on the planet. It couldn't be spelled out more clearly: The way to have the best time as part of the human race is not to get even, but to get odd.

Competition Through The Ages

Ancient Greece   Modern Times

So why are we stuck in the very expensive habit of getting even? Because even our leaders — who already have more than any of us could ever imagine having — still buy into the scare-city mentality. They're scared of losing what they have, and they think the only way to keep from losing is to keep gaining. And no matter how heavy you get, you can never get super-sized enough.

And as you know by now, one of the symptoms of having a Military Industrial Complex is a ravenous appetite where resources are devoured long after the need has passed. And on the other end of things, if you're going to consume that many chemicals and that much fossil fuel, you're gonna have to take a huge toxic dump. There are currently 11,000 military toxic dump sites in this country. The cleaning bill could be between $100 and $200 billion. Our misleaders, having already taken the whole country to the cleaners, are passing that one along to our children and grandchildren.

Here is an odd idea. Maybe we've gone one up as far as we can go. Maybe the smart money is on bringing everyone up instead of the current policies that seem to be bringing everyone down. Right now, some of the best brains on the planet are in someone's employ trying to invent a newer, better way of blowing up people, places and things. Instead of spending one half of our tax revenues looking for even odder ways of getting even, why don't we just call it even and find new ways to get odd? In fact, let's bypass getting even altogether and go right to odd, which is oddly enough, Oneness. Because as three dogs told me one night, "One is the oddest number that you'll ever do."

Now, On the Odder Hand . . .

What if we the people did what was truly unprecedented? How odd would it be if we held ourselves to that One Odd Commandment, the Golden Rule? Instead of being stuck in dueling dualities, why don't we just go for Oneness right off the bat?

First of all, let's get that God is Odd, and so are we. God is

One, and one is as odd as they come. And to paraphrase what God said unto Abraham, "If I'm One, you're one too." Each of us is one-of-a-kind, and maybe the uneven odyssey of life is about expressing our one-of-a-kindness — kindly. And as one-of-a-kind individuals, we each have our own unique expressway to express the peace of God. Which is how each of us becomes a piece of the peace of God. (And by the way, if you think using the word "God" is bad because you've been over-exposed to toxic religion, just laugh and add one of those cheery "o's" to make "God" "Good.")

Yes, being odd is natural. And if we encourage everyone we know to get odd too, then the odds will surely be with us. Now here is something else that's odd. We are being called upon to use our unique set of skills and talents and interests to DO something unusual together, something that has never yet been done: To take charge of our government, and restore our planet to sanity. Not only is this going to take balls, it's going to take oddballs!

As we take the road not yet traveled to do what has never been done, we will be traveling to . . . the unknown. And the best way to prepare for the unknown is by not knowing. There are those who don't know, and don't know they don't know. And not knowing you don't know is no way to go into the unknown, you know. But if you know you don't know, then at least your lack of knowledge will be a known quantity.

Now there is one thing worth knowing once you've figured out you don't know anything, and this is good news. Despite what you know or don't know in your head, in your heart you can know there is a power of Good. So may Good bless you, Good bless me, and Good bless us all as we lead the parade together down the middle of a new road.

From At-Two-Ment to At-One-Ment

Let's face it. Human creativity at its most basic is about putting one and one together and getting . . . one. Each one of us — unless there happens to be an amoeba reading this — is an individual because two individuals came together and — if it was a truly fortuitous moment —came together. Throughout history human couples have coupled not just for the sake of coupling and uncoupling, but to stay hitched to get their offspring sprung off on the right

He's the fruit of our union.

track. And that is good news. The fact that we all came out of labor with a strong union background will help us unite for a common good in the future.

Unfortunately, the world we have been born into is not a union shop. And it's not just that women aren't being paid enough money. It's that they are not being paid enough attention. Now I don't mean to impugn that we don't pay enough attention to Oprah or Baywatch babes, or even Martha Stewart, or that a damsel in distress cannot find a pair of helping hands. No, the women we're not paying attention to are the ones who can help us hear and see what we are not hearing and seeing now.

Because if you look at the male-dominated, stagnated, empty warheads who've got the reins of this stage coach, galloping fool-speed ahead the wrong way down the wrong road, rustling our sacred cows and shouting Jesus' name in vain, we need someone (indeed a world full of someones) to just say "WHOA!"

These lost boys are lost and oblivious to being lost. They don't know that they don't know where they're going, and as missionaries on an Aries mission they wouldn't think to stop and ask directions, and certainly not from a woman. But sometimes what a woman knows, the whole world needs to hear. Mothers know the pain of sacrificing the fruits of their labor to the fruitless labor of deadly combat. Imagine if Boy George had to take his project to the Council of Grandmas. Those vigil aunties would paddle his ass with a spatula and run him right back to his ranch for all that foolishness.

So, another odd question. With the world facing so many challenges right now, doesn't it make sense to draw on all the wisdom on both sides of the yin-yang divide, and not just on the left side of the brain? What kind of dumb-ass Global Brain would dismiss half of its consciousness, particularly if it's the half that could put us in our right mind? *DUH?*

At a time when what isn't working is not just staring us in the eye, it's screaming in our face, wouldn't this be a great opportunity to choose the road not yet taken? Time to march down the middle of a new road together, male and female energies and entities married in a truly empowered coupling. Caring Parents united for the good of all the world's children (and indeed all our relations) offers a lot more than the current Administration's notion of "family values," which in practice more closely resembles "Soprano Family values."

Pro-Creation is Pro-Life for the Living

This is beyond the so-called "pro-life" movement, which is sadly dominated by the dominators. This is the Pro-Creation Movement, a pro-life movement for the live-and-let-living. The Pro-Creation movement favors all loving creations that bring harmony instead of harm. Even those who choose not to bring new children into the world can still give birth to a healthy brainchild — that can bring a new world to our children. Imagine healing forces to turn our karma around, and go the odder way.

Anyone who stayed awake through Alchemistry 1.1 knows the sexual polarities coming together at full strength produces Vitamin Be One, which is a tonic not just to the body politic but to the spirit politic. Vitamin Be One dissolves fear and increases warm electricity between humans. Whether we're in with the yin crowd or down with the yang-bloods (or even a resident of

Was it good for you?

148

Middlesex County), we could all use a boost in electricity. When that synergy doesn't happen, it's a sin.

Vitamin Be One dissolves us all in the One Solution, which is love, yet at the same time we are fully individuated healthy cells operating at capacity. So what does all this have to do with politics? It means getting out of the stag-nation and curing electile dysfunction. Now getting a good strong election sounds like a manly thing, but having the women present and fully-participating will insure a healthy election, sustained long enough to send ripples of pleasure through the entire body politic.

★ PROFILES IN ENCOURAGEMENT

Two Birds of Different Feathers, Flying Together

*A*bout ten years ago, Lynne Twist, an internationally-known fund raiser for nonprofit organizations, traveled to Ecuador and the Amazon rain forest with John Perkins, an environmentalist and naturalist who had worked with shamans in South American for decades. In the course of the trip, Lynne and John and others had the opportunity to participate in a shamanic dream ceremony. Lynne had a memorable and life-changing dream experience. She dreamed she was a large bird flying over a green forest. As she "flew" she saw painted faces adorned with feather crowns floating up towards her. The vivid dream stayed with her for weeks, recurring both in sleep and waking states.

When she described the facial markings and the crown to her friend John Perkins, he recognized them as the markings of Achuar tribe of the Ecuador Amazon. Coincidentally (which seems to be how most incidents are occurring these days), John had recently discovered that the Achuar, after centuries of isolation, were preparing to initiate contact with the modern world about one of the visions they'd been having.

Their dream — actually a common theme among Native peoples of both North and South America — involved two big birds flying as one for the first time: the condor, and the eagle. The condor has long represented the Native peoples to the south. The eagle once represented Native peoples to the north, but now clearly signifies the North American "modern civilization." In their prophetic dreams, the Achuar realized that contact with the modern world was inevitable, and that through "preemptive contact" as equal cultures, they could best preserve their way of life, their wisdom and their rain forest. And in fact, this contact could lead to the fulfillment of the prophecy of the Condor and the Eagle.

Mayan prophecy says in the beginning all of the people on earth were one, but at some point they divided into two paths. The path of the eagle was the path of science, intellect and technology. The path of the condor was intuition and attunement to nature. According to the prophecy, at this point in history the two paths must come back together as one. While the people of the eagle have attained great scientific knowledge and technical know-how that can bring tremendous wealth to the world, there is a poverty of spirit and a disconnection from nature.

Meanwhile, back in the jungle (literally!) the indigenous people have also reached a peak in their intuitive powers, and now can be a valuable resource in creating a sustainable world in tune with all of our relations. Says Lynne in her book, *The Soul of Money,* "The eagle and condor will fly together in the same sky, wing to wing, and the world will come into balance after a point of near extinction."

To help this prophecy come to pass (after all, if the red heifer breeders are trying it, why not us?) Lynne has joined with the Achuar tribe to create the Pachamama Alliance ("pachamama" means "mother earth" in the local language) to help the Achuar choose how to encounter the modern world while preserving the rain forest and "exporting" indigenous wisdom. And that wisdom, coming as it does from a dream culture is simple: "Change the dream."

CHANGING THE DREAM

The Achuar tell us that it is difficult to change daily actions if the old dream is in place. But if we consciously change the dream and tell our vision of the new dream, we can wake up from the current nightmare of mindless fighting over man-made boundaries and unnecessarily scarce resources, and live to cultivate an abundant garden together — each with our own "pachamama" earth to care for.

Forgive — and Forgive Yourself for Not Forgiving Sooner.

Looks like these days, any way you add it up one plus one equals One. Whether it's two lovers, or two cultures or two birds of different feathers, anywhere two or more are gathered, the One shows up. Now that is odd indeed.

But remember, in order for the attunement to at-one-ment to take place, we must dream a new dream, an odd dream, one that will break us of the habit of getting even. Picture this with me. Imagine holding a grudge . . . and then letting it go. Listen, when grudges are held up to the light, we see that they have no talons to grip us with. So when we are in the grip of past conflicts, we are the ones doing the gripping. Let go of your gripping story and drop that grudge now, and watch it fall down the invisible hole into the irretrievable past!

See how easy it is? Isn't it amazing you didn't do it sooner? Don't you feel foolish? Well, we're all foolish, and that's forgivable. In fact, this new dream I'm talking about, this odd and untried approach is called forgiveness. Forgiveness is the weightiness-loss program for the new millennium.

The weightiness we've been gaining is the weight of accumulated grief, injustices and disappointments. These grievances can pile up, creating unsightly build-up on the underside of our karma. Forgiveness is the Creator's soft-cloth karma wash to rinse away all the dirt — including the dirt we've been dishing.

And the more often you visit the karma-wash, the more quickly you'll see your monthly karma payments go down, down, down until the worst you can expect is an occasional bad burrito or unexpected traffic jam. How often you choose to forgive is up to you. If you've been suffering unnecessarily to keep track of an old debt, give up the grievance and you'll save yourself a lot of grief. Then, as long as you pay it no more mind, you're all paid up.

Now just because we forgive a wrong, it doesn't make that wrong right. If it was wrong then, it is still wrong. But when we forgive, we no longer need to hold on to that wrong to remind us how right we are to feel wronged. Eventually, we might give up the grudge, but only begrudgingly. After all, it's our God-given right to be right, right? Well, right. But sometimes being right can be wrong, especially when we're clutching a grudge that just gets heavier and more difficult to carry around.

Look, we've all wronged another, right? And we've all been un-rightly wronged. Great. Let's call it even. Harry Cohen Baba told a Zen Cohen about a village rabbi a hundred years ago. As was the custom, when there was a dispute the disagreeing parties would come to the rabbi for a decision. Whoever lost his case would pay the rabbi. But this one rabbi, noted for his extreme fairness, could never make up his mind. He would listen to the first party, and declare, "You're right." Then he'd listen to the second party and say, "And you're right too."

Consequently, he would leave them agreeing they were both right . . . and would never get paid. After years, his wife had had enough. "Two people come to you in a dispute," she complained, "and you never make a decision. You say, 'you're right' and 'you're right', they leave and you never get paid!"

The rabbi sighed. "And you're right too."

So I'm right, you're right, we're all right. And if we're *all* all right . . . well, it must be all right!

So forgive yourself. And forgive yourself for not forgiving yourself sooner. When it comes to happiness in life, forgiveness is a given. Not forgiving is unforgivable.

A Few Odd Solutions to the Problem of Getting Even

What if the nations of the world made a commitment to get odd instead of getting even? Sounds ridiculous? Maybe so, but it's a heaven-of-a-lot better than what we've been doing.

1. Send the World Leaders to Confession.
Name me a country that has done no harm, and I'll show you a nameless country. Because every country that has a name has some kind of black mark next to it. On that account, we're all even. So an odd thing would be, what if every world leader had to go to confession to confess the sins of his or her country? Think of all that collective guilt we could collect in one place — and dispose of without releasing harmful toxins into the atmosphere.

We have a perfectly good Pope — let's use him, for Goodness sakes! All nations, all religions, all institutions, it is time to declare moral bankruptcy and ask for forgiveness. Imagine world leaders going to the Vatican, and walking into that small confessional weighed down by the burdens of history, and walking out as light as an angel fart. My personal opinion is, confession is one of the best things the Catholic Church has going, and more people need to participate in this healing practice.

Maybe on Yom Kippur, the Jewish Day of At-One-Ment, the Catholic Church can open its doors to the entire community and hold a "forgiveness sale": "Confess now, and we'll make your next karma payment for you!" I also encourage the church to forgive divorce and promote ex-communication. After all, the better we communicate with our "ex", the easier forgiveness will be all around.

And of course the church must confess and forgive itself as well, not just for all those burnt sages centuries ago, but for insisting that the only form of population control must be copulation control, and then covering up the "Leave No Child's Behind" program that far too many priests were running in far too many communities.

The same goes for every one of us. All religions, all nations, all races. 'Fess up! We know you did it. We all did it! *Mea culpa, you-a culpa, we all-a culpa!* Forgive us, Father, for we have sinned. That's right, we have all wronged, and been wronged. So let's confess and forgive. Forgiveness is a rite of right-being that can set right any wrongdoing.

2. Establish The Iraqifeller Fund Peace Prize.

Might as well admit it. We made a mess in Mesopotamia. But as mom always told us, if you're going to make a mess, you have to clean it up. So let's get to work. I know a lot of soldiers have been doing some soldier-searching in the wake of revelations about prison treatment. They're starting to admit to themselves, "Yeah, I guess we were pretty hard on those Iraqi fellers."

And that is why I propose the Iraqifeller Fund as an odd alternative to getting even. Quite simply, the fund would offer a $10 billion prize — equally apportioned to every man, woman and child in Iraq — if they establish a pluralistic government, refrain from killing members of the opposite sects, and live by the Golden Rule of law for one year. The first prize — awarded immediately — is the U.S. and Coalition Forces returning home. That's a win for everyone. Then it's up to them. Now I know that this sounds like something Pat Buchanan presented a while back, but I can't help it if Pat Buchanan is right from time to time.

As a variation of the not-yet-produced reality TV show, "Thrivor!" Iraqis would receive support from the outside world and be cheered on each week on network TV. Maybe we could even give our toady protégé, Achmed Chalabi his own TV show, just to keep him occupied and out of trouble. We could pair him with another former world leader, and the two of them could use the show to begin paying the world back for what was lost investing in the Iraqi Horror Picture Show. I'm serious. Who wouldn't tune in to watch The Adventures of Iraqi and Bushwinkle?

I see the Iraqis getting fan mail to encourage them in their endeavors. In fact, in an outpouring of support for the Iraqi people, I see Americans holding bake sales, and sending the proceeds to Iraq — along with the baked goods. Hey, we're fat enough to sue McDonald's. What do we need with more fattening desserts?

Yes, I see Operation Dessert Storm as an important message to the people of Iraq. Everyone in the world deserves sweetness in their lives, so we are simply giving them their just desserts to make up for years of sadness. And you know what? Everybody in the world who wants peace and justice will be rooting for the Iraqis because they figure, if the Iraqis can pull this off, anyone can!

3. Practice FUNdamentalism — Accent on "Fun".

So it's finally come to this. The Swami's agenda is revealed, and he's selling a new religion. Mea culpa, again. But this is a religion not to be taken seriously, where the accent is on fun, and where the worship takes the form of laughter.

Look at all those fundaMENTAList religions up in their heads, and their heads up you-know-where. They are obsessed with getting even. An eye for an eye. But we FUNdamentalists see it the odder way around. We say, laugh and let laugh. HA!

You're laughing. Well, don't laugh. If the terrorists had comedy, would they be blowing themselves up? Listen, when a comedian kills, the audience ends up more alive than when they came in. Explain that.

Do you realize that every day, millions with spiritual hunger seeking soul-food are lured into some unhealthy spiritual fast-food joint because they're hungry and those are the only shops on the strip? All of those fundaMENTAList groups have their out-reach, so why shouldn't we FUNdamentalists do in-reach? That is where we reach into someone's heart and belly and pull out a good laugh. Now you're probably saying, wait a minute. There are all those situation comedies and funny reality TV shows. It seems like there's plenty to laugh at. Yes, but only if you believe in the tickle down theory.

Much of the fun we see others having on TV doesn't tickle down. We need to have present and direct experiences of the laugh force in our own lives to truly feel the levitational pull to help us lighten up. Now we FUNdamentalists aren't out there trying to save souls. We're just trying to help souls spend themselves more wise-ly. So here are some cosmic comic practices to get others who are not yet having fun to say, "I'll have what (s)he's having!"

√ **Commit Random Acts of Comedy.** Ask the telemarketer who calls to tell you a joke, and then tell that joke to the next tele-marketer. Next time you're at a conference, creatively re-arrange the plastic letters on the events marquee. Do no harm. Whatever you do, don't, *don't*, **don't** put bubble bath in the fountains in front of your office building!

√ **Practice Fun-Shui.** Fun-Shui is the art of arranging items to elicit a smile, if not an outright guffaw. Home and work spaces with good fun-shui have plenty of stuffed animal cartoon char-acters, rubber yellow duckies, and other playful surprises strewn in a laugh-enhancing fashion. You'll know you've successfully created a farce-field when jokes materialize by themselves, and people begin laughing for no reason.

√ **Commit Hokey Pokey.** We all do and say foolish things. (If you are saying, "Not me," I rest my case.) The fooly-realized ones real-ize that foolishness is a human trait, manifested regularly. So why should we take our mistakes seriously? We could be like those poor sushi chefs. When they blow it on a blowfish, causing some patron to check out before the check, they must commit hari-kari.

But the foo ling master celebrates his mistake in an orgy of fool-realization by committing Hokey Pokey. He or she gathers any crowd around, puts their whole self in, and invites everyone to laugh at their foolish mistake. This is proven to be good karma. Whenever anyone laughs at our expense, the Eternal Revenue Services takes it off of our karmic expense account. And you know the old saying: Laugh at yourself, and the whole world will laugh at you too.

√ **Join the Million Clown March.** If you just can't stand sitting still while our current misleaders goose-step us toward Armageddon, then change the route of the parade 180 degrees, and help march us toward Disarmageddon instead. Yes, there is a Million Clown March, a million and one if you join. Read all about it in the Resources and Recourses section just up ahead. If you want to throw all seriousness to the wind and become a comic-kazi, then join these pie-in-the-face pioneers. But please, no pie in the ears.

Are You Ready for Nonjudgment Day?

I have a dream. I have a dream of Disarmageddon and Nonjudgment day, a day of civil discourse when the Elephant lies down with the Donkey . . . and doesn't roll over on top of him. I have a dream that the leaders of the world will all commit Hokey Pokey together at the U.N., and the forces of laughter will become greater than the farces of negativity, criticism and judgment. With no one criticizing, we will have uncritical mass and — it goes without saying — Nonjudgment Day. Now this may sound like some wild, pie-in-the-face vision, but I ask you: Which world would you choose to live in? The world where we dance the Hokey Pokey together, or the one where we blow each other up?

The choice is ours every day and every minute . . . love or fear. Will we continue down the well-worn path to Armageddon . . . or take the road less traveled to Disarmageddon instead? Are we going to buy into original sin, or go for humanifest destiny where we actually realize our human potential? Because no matter what I see on the 6 o'clock news I believe we have the potential to be human, that mankind can treat man kindly, and that we can bring about Nonjudgment Day where all heaven will break loose!

May we laugh, laugh, laugh till the sacred cows come home. For truly the farce is with us.

---⭐---

SWAMI ANSWERS YOUR QUESTIONS . . . AND YOU WILL QUESTION HIS ANSWERS.

Will Gay Marriage Lead to Gay Divorcees?

Dear Swami:

What is it with these gay people and their gay rights? I'm sorry, but with everything going on, I'm not sure I'd want gays in the military. And really. Marriage is about one man and one woman, always has been and always will be. Otherwise, it ain't marriage, it's something else. In short, Swami, what is this world coming to? And why the hell am I asking you, anyway?

—*Dickson Frundt,*
Raytown, Missouri

Dear Dickson:

Yes, it is true times are changing. After all, gay people are coming into their own, are they not? And it is understandable they'd want the right to do anything anyone else could do, including become Republican. In fact, there is an entire organization of Gay Republicans called the Log Cabin Republicans (presumably named because of the link with Lincoln). But many Republicans nowadays have become so unlinked from Lincoln, they very likely don't understand the reference, and probably think it refers to linkin' logs, something no self-respecting Republican would dream of doing with another Republican.

Meanwhile, the Log Cabin group recently reassured the President they were behind him, and planned to back him all the way. The President, however, declined their backing, saying it put him in "an awkward position." President Bush did say that he supported gays in the military, but in a "limited capacity." He said, "You know those decorated soldiers? Well, I guess we do need someone to actually decorate them."

In regards to marriage, I can see your point that matrimony is for one man and one woman, but how about those harems? Or the old-time Mormons? But maybe there is an odd solution that will satisfy the traditionalists, and eager gay couples willing to take the plunge and risk becoming gay divorcees down the line. I suggest that when two men choose to establish a lifelong bond, let us call it Fratrimony. And when two women tie the knot, let it be in Galimony. In a world where fear and hatred seem to have hold of the megaphone, let us all celebrate and nourish love wherever and however it springs up, even if we don't choose to watch that love being consummated on some webcam.

Use the Third Way to Get Odd

Dear Swami:

What do you do when folks are simply stuck in positions, like the abortion issue. Seems like folks are either on one side or the other, with no ground in between. Any ideas?

—Blair Lowdleigh,
Charlottesville, Virginia

Dear Blair,

Well, when there is no middle ground, the idea is to get both parties to look up so they're both seeing the same thing at the same time. When you're stuck in dueling dualities, maybe you need to offer a third way to break the tie. Like those three religious leaders on TV discussing when life begins. "Life begins at the moment of conception," said the priest.

"No, life begins at birth," said the minister.

"You're both wrong," said the rabbi. "Life begins when the children leave home and the dog dies."

Two Ideas to Even Up the Odds
for Peace in the Middle East

Dear Swami:

It seems like it all comes down to the Middle East. We have the Israelis and Palestinians deadlocked, and the prospects for peace diminishing. Clearly, getting even hasn't worked. But Swami, is there some odd solution we're not seeing that is cause for hope?

—Farrakhan A. Wright,
Chicago, Illinois

Dear Farrakhan,

I've got good news, and I've got good news. I have an even number of odd solutions to try, one to work on the physical, the other on the metaphysical plane. First, the physical. Now I have been praying about this issue for a long time, taking the question into the higher states. On my last trip to the higher states, I actually went even further north, beyond Minnesota even, to Canada. And I think our Canadian neighbors might have the answer. The Canadians don't shoot each other. They have a very low crime rate. They are the most peaceful, civilized people in the world, except for one thing . . . hockey.

So that is my simple plan for peace in the Middle East: Hockey! Little Palestinian kids, little Israeli kids channeling thousands of years of frustration into hockey. Hamas vs. Mosad at Madison Square Garden. They could charge admission and raise money for peace organizations. You can bet there's gonna be some high-sticking and crosschecking, but you know what? It beats the hell out of suicide bombing and homicide retaliation, and once and for all, it's a way to put the entire conflict on ice.

On the metaphysical side, it is heartening to know we have helpers in the beyond. I was cruising the higher planes last year, and you know, you never know who you're going to sit next to. I'm sitting next to this guy, and he looks very familiar but I can't place him. Finally, I say, "You look really familiar."

And he says, "Yes, I'm George Gershwin."

And I say, "George Gershwin, the composer?"

He says, "Yes."

So I asked him what he was doing these days.

"Decomposing," replied the dead composer. But then he said that he really cared about the healing of this planet, and that he was particularly saddened that the Israelis and the Palestinians had almost the same word for peace, but couldn't seem to create peace to save their lives. And then he brightened. "Would you be willing to take my healing message to that part of the world?" he asked.

Well, how could I turn down the guy who wrote "Swami, How I Love Ya?" So here is George Gershwin's song for peace in the Middle East:

Let's Call the Old Thing Off

You say salaam, and I say shalom
You throw a bomb, I blow up your home
Salaam! Shalom! We blow up our home
Oh, let's call the old thing off

You say baraka, I say barucha
I spin the dreidl, you toke the hookah
Barucha, baraka . . . this warfare is ca-ca
Let's call the old thing off

And oh, if we call the old thing off we'll both be right
And if we both are right, well there's no need to fight

I eat the kasha, you eat the kibbe
We both dig falafel, but never pork ribbie
To kasha! To kibbe! Forget the pork ribbie
(At least there's one thing we agree on)

Haven't we had enough?
Let's call the old thing off
Th-th-th-th-that's all, folks!

But Seriously, Folks . . .

What would happen if we tried something odder than getting even? What if we applied our human intelligence on behalf of something intelligent for a change?

Sure, it's a challenge to give peace a chance, but don't you think war has already taken way too many shots — and missed? Are you satisfied with unnecessary suffering, or ready to take a chance on something new?

What if children of God everywhere finally grew up, and became adults of God, aware and enlightened co-creators choosing love and not fear?

The World Game — Wouldn't this be a great family game for the whole to world to play? And you know what they say. A family that plays together, stays together.

Let the games begin!

SWAMI BEYONDANANDA'S DICTIONARY of AMERICAN POLITICS FROM A TO Z

ABunDance: Creating sufficiency by getting up off our assets, moving our buns, and dancing to the music of the spheres. A great way to overcome fear of not having enough, or *Scare-City.*

Absurdification: A piece of paper that proudly proclaims one's foolishness and the willingness to laugh at that foolishness by taking a vow of levity. See *Fool-Realization.*

Againstum: The opposite of *forum.* The normal way of approaching problems by butting heads. Those who no longer want to be butt-heads say, "We need more forums and fewer againstums. See *Buttal.*

Age of Nefarious: A transitional stage right before the Age of Aquarius. Said to begin "when the goon moves into Lincoln's house and stupider aligns with Mars," and said to end when we let the sunlight of transparency, love and laughter shine in.

Alter-Native Economy: Where we invest in goods and services instead of bads and disservices, and we natives are altered for the better.

American Devolution, The: A degenerative condition of the body politic that has caused us to go from fighting taxation without representation to **not** fighting representation without taxation. See *Incontinental Congress.*

American Evolution, The: The next stage in becoming the sovereign citizens our Founding Fathers imagined, it will begin on Election Day when the first Big Shot is fired.

Anti-Defecation League, The: An organization dedicated to protecting non-terrorists who find themselves on government shit-lists. See *Irony Curtain*.

Assaholism: A laugh-threatening delusional state where sufferers actually believe the Earth revolves around them. Can result in an addiction to getting one's own way at all costs. See *Ignoranus*.

Banana Republicans: A cadre of Republicans (and some Democrats) disguised as public servants, who are serving themselves first, their cronies second and the people last. So named because their policies are turning our republic into a Banana Republic. See *Gold Collar Criminals*.

Bill Clinton: A President whose little peccadillo got blown all out of proportion. Meanwhile, Bush was in bed with a Lay who screwed millions.

Bill Of Wrongs: See *USA Patriot Act*.

Blisskrieg: Swami's world win campaign to generate enough love, joy and laughter to bring about Disarmageddon and Nonjudgment day. Why wait from a bail out from above? This is supply-side spirituality! See *Disarmageddon*.

Bomb-A-Nation, A: A deadly sin not recognized as such by the Religious Right.

Born Feed-Us: What happens to an unborn fetus when it gets born and needs to be fed.

Boston TV Party: One of the key incidents of the American Evolution, where a band of patriots decide to toss their TV's and tell a vision instead.

Bozone Layer: The delicate laugh force around our planet caused by rising levity; the planetary *Clown Chakra*.

Buttal: An argumentative opening statement that invites a rebuttal.

Calm-Petition: A peaceful prayerful state where every soul gets heard.

Candid Karma: The hilarious human follies show that God enjoys so much, it will never be cancelled.

Ch'i Ting: Ancient Chinese practice of using energy field, or "ch'i" (pronounced "chee") to gain unfair advantage. In the current cover-your-ass environment, it is used to stretch the law to cover even the biggest ass.

CityZen Union: A local group that brings together people from all viewpoints to meditate peacefully and create solutions that none of them could have come up with on their own.

Clown Chakra: An energy center that opens one up to the higher powers of levity. Can sometimes be seen in evolved foo ling masters as a bright reddish glow in front of the nose.

Code Green: An emerge 'n see measure where we emerge from the habit of getting even, and find the healing odd solution just ridiculous enough to work.

Columbo's Day: A proposed holiday where citizens emulate the great TV detective and ask unasked questions and question unquestioned answers.

Cootie État: Causing a regime change by focusing only on the miniscule faults of the incumbent. See *Bill Clinton.*

Deadlihood: A deadly condition of the neighborhood due to the absence of livelihood. Swami says, "if we want to turn a deadly 'hood into a lively 'hood, the neighbors must be stronger in force than the hoods — and the promise of livelihood must be greater than the profits of deadlihood."

Deficit Inattention Disorder: A condition of the body politic — thought to be exacerbated by large doses of mass media — which weakens the consumer's resistance with a barrage of advertising, while credit card companies feed on them to make sure they buy, buy, buy until it's bye-bye money. See *Near-Debt Experience.*

Democrats: A political party, supposedly representing the people, that has suffered electile dysfunction because of an inability to get hard. Political theme song has switched in recent years from "Don't Stop Thinking About Tomorrow" to "It's My Party and I'll Cry If I Want To."

Demagogue: A divisionary who spews impropaganda blaming "dem," and never "us."

De-Tex: A necessary cleanse of the body politic to heal chemical dependency (especially those chemicals based on fossil fuels), and overcome Mad Cowboy Disease.

Disarmageddon: The inevitable day when we humans finally lay down our arms. We will look pretty foolish with our arms on the ground and our butts sticking up in the air, but you know what? You cannot attack anyone in that position.

Divisionaries: Those who benefit by keeping the rest of stuck in dueling dualities and getting even.

Dogma-Doo: The mess that dogmas leave behind that we've been stepping into for centuries.

Downheaval: Compared to downheaval, upheaval is definitely the lesser of two heavals.

Electile Dysfunction: Failure to sustain an election, due to an inability to get hard. See *Democrats.*

Elvis's Witnesses: A religious sect that goes door-to-door presleytizing and asking, "Are you lonesome tonight?" See *Presleyterianism.*

Emerge 'N See Measures: Unlike "emergency" which is activated by fear, an emerge 'n see is a heightened awareness activated by love.

Empowerhouse: An energetic individual who empowers others by causing their esteem to rise. *See esteem generator.*

Esteem-Generator: Someone who helps generate esteem through love and laughter.

Eternal Revenue Service: An intergalactic agency that keeps track of karma payments. Remember when your teachers used to say, "This will go on your permanent record?" This is what they were talking about.

Ethic Cleansing: The removal of scrupulous people from a government agency, so that illegal activities can continue unencumbered.

F-Word, The: A euphemism for the unspeakable, Fascism, a loathsome disease of the body politic where all the tissue turns to muscle, and the heart is squeezed like a lemon. See *Not-Seeism.*

Farce Fields: Energy field where jokes mysteriously appear. See *Bozone layer.*

Feariority Complex: A state of mind that keeps the body politic in scare-city, and easy to manipulate.

Foo Ling Masters: Fooly-realized beings who laugh wholeheartedly at their foolishness, and teach others to do the same.

Fool-Realization: The elevated state of levity where one is able to laugh lovingly at one's foolishness.

Fratrimony: The legal term for two men marrying so that matrimony can be preserved for heterosexuals.

Fun Doo: A FUNdamentalist practice (accent on "fun") where you actually enjoy what you're doing and do what you enjoy.

FUNdamentalist: New religion sweeping the world where the accent is on "fun." Proof that you can teach an old dogma new tricks.

Fun Shui: The arrangement of stuffed animals and other playful items to create a farce-field and elicit laughter.

Fung Shun: The ancient and revered practice of living daily life. Where the karma meets the road.

Galimony: The legal term for two women marrying so that matrimony can be preserved for heterosexuals.

Gobble-ization: The practice of mining the global economy (by saying, "mine, mine, mine") so that greedy turkeys gobble everything up.

Goebbelization: The practice of using impropaganda world-wide to justify gobble-ization.

Gold-Collar Criminals: High-level criminals clever enough to collar the gold without getting collared themselves.

Greedlock: In government, the inability to pass beneficial legislation because the greedy parties have a lock on members of both parties. See *Gold Collar Crime.*

Happy Medium: In this dogma-eat-dogma world, what most peace loving people are looking for, and Swami Beyondananda fits the bill. He's one of the happiest mediums around.

Humanifest Destiny: Where we achieve our human potential as mankind learns to treat man kindly.

Ignoranus: Massive ignorance meets massive arrogance, wrapped up in one individual. See *Assaholism.*

Imaginot Line: The imaginary line that our government crosses when it limits freedom of imagination.

Impropaganda: Misinformation, disinformation and missing information that keeps the Irony Curtain in place.

Incarcenoma: A potentially-deadly condition where prisons proliferate throughout the body politic where schools used to be.

Incontinental Congress: Current batch of legislators pissing away our Constitutional rights by being enablers for an Administration perpetrating unconstitutional wrongs. See *Banana Republicans.*

Iraqifeller Fund, The: A $10 billion prize to be shared by every Iraqi man, woman and child if they're able to survive a year governing themselves without warfare. Money donated by the U.S. to make up for mess in we made in Mesopotamia.

Irony Curtain: An invisible wall of impropaganda that has come down to separate the body politic from the truth.

Irony Deficiency: A disease of the body politic caused by a mass media that inundates us with so much toxic B. S. that our skeptic system overflows and we end up swallowing huge ironies whole. Seeing a doctor won't help, but seeing a paradox will.

Irony Supplement: Little bits of news or sound bites so rich in irony that they cause explosions of laughter, followed by awakening and insight.

Karma Payments: Accounts receivable for past transgressions. See *Eternal Revenue Service.*

Law of Grabbity: A man-made illegal law that says whoever has the biggest hand and the strongest arm can grab anything they want.

Levitational Pull: The pull of cosmic laughter to counteract the forces of gravity, it is the force that causes the corners of the mouth to turn upward in a smile.

Mad Cowboy Disease: A toxic condition of affecting the head of state that causes the body politic to go into a state of cattlepsy and drift into the bewilderness. See *De-Tex.*

Man Hog Day: The day the body politic sees it's shadow, votes accordingly, and prevents four more years of darkness.

Manhelpin Project: A "Manhattan Project" to develop clean, renewable "new clear energy," and help the planet achieve fuel-realization.

Mass-Debating: The habit we have of endless arguing instead of having a loving intercourse where we produce a beautiful brainchild together.

Mental Floss: A practice designed to clear the mind and prevent truth decay. Should be done at least once daily, twice during Republican administrations. See *Truth Decay.*

Military Industrial Complex: An obsessive and compulsive disorder of the body politic, where a society's wealth is hoarded and hidden behind defense.

Mockracy: A toxic mimic of the inspired system devised by Jefferson, Madison and company where the government does the bidding of the highest bidder, and makes a mockery of our highest principles. See *USA Patriot Act*.

Near-Debt Experience: A life-changing event when sufferers of Deficit Inattention Disorder and Military Industrial Complex see the light, and turn away from a debt-end road.

Needy-Greedy: The ancient and persistent struggle for money that comes from fear of not having enough. See *Scare-City*.

No Bull Prize, The: An award given each year to a courageous individual who tells the truth in a political system where lie-ability is an asset.

Nomad Lifestyle: A healthy lifestyle choice where we stop holding grudges and leave the baggage of the past behind. Characterized by the "Nomad Credo," — I no mad at you, you no mad at me — it may be the key for having nomadness on the planet.

Nonjudgment Day: A time when enough humans stop criticizing one another, that we achieve uncritical mass. A day when everyone wins beauty contests, and all lawyers disappear because our trials are over. See *Disarmageddon*.

Not-Seeism: A dangerous state of denial where, despite all of the evidence, people insist on not seeing the truth. See *F-Word*.

Ombuddhasman: An individual, hired by a business or an agency, to ask the question, "What would Buddha do?" and help all parties involved find the odd solution instead of merely getting even.

One One One: A counter-celebration to the 9/11 attack, we celebrate January 11th as the day we remember what God said to Abraham: "If I'm One, you're one too!"

Operation Dessert Storm: A mobilization of bake sales throughout the U.S. to bring sweetness into the lives of long-suffering Iraqis and give them their just desserts. See *Iraqifeller Fund.*

Optimystic: A mystic who places belief in human potential instead of original sin, and says, "No matter what I see on the news, I still believe we have the potential to be human." See *Pessimystic.*

Pessimystic: The pessimystics are very much in touch with reality, but the optimystics are happier and live longer for some reason. Pessimystics insist the sky is falling. Optimystics say it only looks that way because we are ascending. See *Optimystic.*

Pocket Protectorate: A city, country or area adopted by the entire world and protected from warfare.

Pray-Offs: Also known as the God-Will Games, it is a calm-petition to celebrate all forms of healing prayer.

Presleyterianism: A religion based on the Three Commandments of Elvis: Love Me Tender. Please Surrender. Return to Sender. See *Elvis's Witnesses.*

Pro-Creation Movement: A pro-life movement for the live-and-let-living, it favors all loving creations bringing harmony instead of harm.

Propheteering: The practice — seen in some circles as highly unethical — of making predictions for money.

Quid Pro Quo Pro: Someone who trades political favors for money. A politician.

Ramparts: Forget those ramparts unless you happen to be a sheep. We have been ramming parts for far too long.

Right-To-Laugh Party: Political movement created to counteract the laugh-threatening seriousness of both terrorism and anti-terrorism. Their slogan is, "One big party, everyone is invited . . . All for fun, and fun for all."

Safe Sects: Sects entered into by mutually-consenting adults, that promote sects equality.

Scare-City: The fear of not having enough that keeps us fighting to get even instead of finding the odd solution that will bring A-Bun-Dance. See *A-Bun-Dance.*

Selfish-Righteousness: A condition, usually occurring on the right side of the body politic, where righteousness is used to mask selfishness.

Sinatra Syndrome: Also known as a "doo-be-doo-be-doo" imbalance, a condition that usually involves not enough being and too much doing.

Skeptic System: The part of the human jestive system that breaks down toxic ironies into solid truth, and releases bubbles of laughter that improve the atmosphere.

Smartyrdom: A smarter-than-thou attitude which makes it difficult to compromise. It is how the Left got left, and consequently how the Right got right.

Spendex: A space-age substance which all new money will be made of to allow us to stretch the dollar like never before.

Stag-nation: A condition where the body politic is so over-run with butt-heads butting heads that nothing healthy can move forward.

Sue-widge: The toxic detritus caused by an overflow of lawsuits and the malfunction of our skeptic systems.

Supply-Side Spirituality: A form of do-it-yourself home planet improvement, an alternative to waiting for a bail-out from above.

Supreme Court Jester: An individual empowered to tell the truth when no one else can. Most Americans would agree there's definitely something funny going on, so who better to deal with it?

Tanksgiving: A holiday which commemorates America's long and glorious history of arming the forces of repression worldwide.

Tantrum Yoga: An ancient Vedic technique for using anger to heat your home.

Tell-A-Vision: A key to changing the current programming is to turn off your TV and tell a vision instead. This enables us to step into a healing, empowering vision — which beats what we've been stepping into lately.

Tell-A-Person: A recently rediscovered ancient form of communication that can turn the masses into the media.

Thrival: The stage beyond survival where we all weave a web of mass-construction and reap a world win.

Tickle-Down Theory: The now-discredited notion that laughter in the highest echelons of society will naturally make it's way down from the hierarchy to the lowerarchy.

Transcendentists: Those who have learned to use mental floss to prevent truth decay.

Truth Decay: Progressive truth loss due to the effects of assaholism, and toxic media. See *Irony Curtain.*

Uncommontators: People like Michael Moore, Arianna Huffington, Jim Hightower and Greg Palast, who tell the truth and ask the crucial questions in the media.

Uncritical Mass: When enough people on the planet choose to laugh instead of criticize, the Swami says, "we will achieve the uncritical mass needed to bring about Nonjudgment Day." See *Nonjudgment Day.*

USA Patriot Act: A serious symptom of irony deficiency and truth decay, it is an unconstitutional piece of legislation designed to turn our national motto into, "One nation, under guard."

Vigil Aunties: Those tough-as-nail prayin' women of the wild west who made sure there was some kind of Universal Law west of the Pecos.

Vitamin Be One: An invisible substance that allows us to dissolve all difficulties in a warm solution of love.

Votee: A spiritual devotee who expresses consciousness by coming down to the physical plane long enough to vote.

War on Terra: The ongoing pursuit of wealth at any cost that has overmined, and consequently undermined our planet.

Wealthfair: A radical new program to help rich and poor alike become fairly wealthy and wealthy fairly, and create a-bun-dance by getting up off their assets and dancing together to create real wealth that benefits all.

Xavier Onassis: Cousin of famed Greek shipping magnate, he was the first to articulate the survivalist philosophy.

Yearning Disability: Inability to imagine a better future, caused by too much TV and not enough tell-a-vision.

Zen Cohen, A: Configuration of words designed to elicit a moment enlightenment with a spark of laughter.

To find more words . . . or nominate some words of your own,
go to Swami's Dictionary at www.wakeuplaughing.com.

Resources & Recourses

Check this page at
www.wakeuplaughing.com
for hot links and updated
information.

Introduction

Who stole the kishka?
According to the website below, in the fiscal year 2001, the
Department of Defense found $1.1 trillion in "unsupported
accounting entries," which in accounting language means
"missing money."
http://www.whereisthemoney.org/1.1trillion.htm

What would Jefferson do?
Regarding Thomas Jefferson, one of the best sources
is Thom Hartmann, whose new book is out this July 4th.
Thom Hartmann, *What Would Jefferson Do? : A Return to
Democracy*. Random House /Harmony, 2004.
http://www.thomhartmann.com

Chapter One. Let's Elect Ourselves.

Information on why Nobody won in 2000.
International Voter Turnout, 1991-2000
http://www.fairvote.org/turnout/intturnout.htm

Votes cast for Presidential Candidates
http://www.fairvote.org/turnout/prevote2000.htm

How America's gone whole hog.
International Consumption
http://www.newdream.org/intl/

Population and Consumption
http://www.sierraclub.org/population/consumption/

From the monkey mind to the hundredth monkey mind.
Eckhart Tolle, *The Power of Now,* New World Library, 1999.
http://www.eckharttolle.com/mainpage.htm

Hundredth Monkey
http://www.worldtrans.org/pos/monkey.html

Notes on the world's other super power.
Worldwide War Protest - March 2003
http://people.cornellcollege.edu/a-free/feb15.htm

Robert Muller. Antiwar thinking: Taking comfort in remarkable footholds gained
http://www.csmonitor.com/2003/0320/p11s01-coop.html

From American Revolution to American Evolution . . .
Thom Hartmann, *What Would Jefferson Do? : A Return to Democracy.* Random House /Harmony, 2004.
http://www.thomhartmann.com

US Constitution
http://www.usconstitution.net/

Voting and the paper trail . . .
. . . and not just the one you accidentally
track in from the bathroom.
http://www.verifiedvoting.org/
http://www.blackboxvoting.com

The Center for Voting and Democracy
http://www.fairvote.org/

Project VoteSmart
http://www.vote-smart.org/

Chapter Two. Improve Reality.

Who wants to feed the wolf of peace?
Paul H. Ray, Ph.D. and Sherry Ruth Anderson, Ph.D. *The Cultural Creatives: How 50 Million People Are Changing the World,* Harmony Books, 2000.
http://www.culturalcreatives.org/

The high cost of paying the ultimate price:
Cost of War
http://costofwar.com/

The Defense Budget And Wartime Profiteering
http://www.tompaine.com/feature2.cfm/ID/6469

Fiscal Year 2004 Military Spending
http://www.cdi.org/budget/2004/world-military-spending.cfm

High Military Expenditure
http://www.globalissues.org/Geopolitics/ArmsTrade/Spending.asp

And the cost of not investing in the Be One:
Air Force Grounds Fleet of B2 Bombers
http://www.cnn.com/US/9808/06/b2.grounded/

The B2 Bomber
http://www.clw.org/milspend/b2_1999.html

Find out about the World Game here.
Buckminster Fuller Institute
http://www.bfi.org/introduction_to_bmf.htm

And healing laughter.
Norman Cousins
http://www.harvardsquarelibrary.org/unitarians/cousins.html

Join the Right to Laugh Party . . .
http://www.righttolaugh.com

For a comprehensive program to improve reality . . .
Da Vid, The Light Party.
http://www.lightparty.com

Chapter Three. Pray It Forward.

Shoot Out at the I'm OK You're _Not_ OK Corral.
Armageddon: The Diabolical God of Christian and Jewish
Zionists (NEW) by Grace Halsel
http://www.grecoreport.com/armageddon.htm

Holy Cow!
Holy cow! Will red heifer save world, cattle industry?
http://www.jewishsf.com/content/2-0-/module/displaystory/
    story_id/6533/edition_id/122/format/html/displaystory.html

A shrink for a shrinking world?
Milton Rokeach, _The Three Christs of Ypsilanti_,
Random House Trade Paperbacks, 1964.
http://www3.uakron.edu/ahap/rokeach_m.htm

E Pluribus Unum!
The Universality of the Golden Rule in the World Religions
http://www.teachingvalues.com/goldenrule.html

Pray it forward!
Larry Dossey, _Prayer is Good Medicine: How to Reap the Healing
Benefits of Prayer_, Harper San Francisco, 1996.
http://www.dosseydossey.com/larry/default.html

Resources for universal spirituality and political awareness.
Sojourners
http://www.sojo.net/

Tikkun
http://www.tikkun.org/

Meditation Station
http://www.meditationsociety.com/
Prayer Circles
http://www.beliefnet.com/prayer/commemoration.asp?
    milestoneTypeID=6&milestoneID=2781

Resources for Peace
http://www.givewings.com/peace/linkspage.html

For an interesting perspective on science and love . . .
A Japanese doctor offers photos of water crystals that were
"loved" and others that were "hated" . . . check it out.
http://www.whatthebleep.com/crystals/

And another helpful book on the power of love
Glenda Green, *Love Without End,* Heartwings Publishing, 1999.
http://www.lovewithoutend.com/

Chapter Four. Tell-A-Vision

American Banned Stand Charts.
Clear Channel Banned Songs
http://radio.about.com/library/weekly/blCCbannedsongs.htm

How news gets manufactured.
General Electric
http://www.hoovers.com/ge/—ID__10634—/free-co-subs.xhtml

Smart planet, foolish choices . . .
Was inspired by reading this book, Thom Hartmann, *Last
Hours of Ancient Sunlight, Three Rivers Press*, 2004.
http://www.thomhartmann.com

Putting intelligent life on earth.
Apollo Alliance
http://www.apolloalliance.org/

Greenpeace Clean Energy Now
http://www.cleanenergynow.org/

Destination Imagination
http://www.destinationimagination.org/

Chapter Five. Invest in A-Bun-Dance, Not Scare-City.

Tracking the drug dealers.
Pharmaceutical Research and Manufacturers Association
http://www.disinfopedia.org/wiki.phtml?title=Pharmaceutical_
   Research_and_Manufacturers_of_America

The Other Drug War II
http://www.citizen.org/congress/reform/drug_industry/
   contribution/articles.cfm?ID=7827
Brand-Name Drug Companies versus Generics:

Campaign and Lobbying Contributions
http://www.citizen.org/congress/reform/drug_industry/
   contribution/articles.cfm?ID=8045

Drug Industry Poised to Reap Political Dividends
http://www.commondreams.org/headlines02/1108-02.htm

Pay, Profits and Spending by Drug Companies
http://www.actupny.org/reports/drugcosts.html

Spending More Than a Half Billion on Political Contributions
http://www.commoncause.org/action/070103_phrma_report.pdf

Representation without taxation.
David Cay Johnston. *Perfectly Legal: The Covert Campaign to
Rig Our Tax System to Benefit the Super Rich and Cheat
Everybody Else* (Portfolio, 2003).
http://www.fairness.com/resources/by-relation?relation_id=7663
http://www.perfectlylegalthebook.com/
http://www.buzzflash.com/interviews/04/03/int04016.html
http://www.forbes.com/ceonetwork/2004/02/12/
   0212chat_transcript.html

Gold Collar Crime: Follow the gold . . .
http://www.makethemaccountable.com/podvin/media/
020203_MissingOverall.htm

Deficit Inattention Disorder reality check point
US National Debt Clock
http://www.brillig.com/debt_clock/

Cradle to Cradle: It's the ecology, and it's the economy.
William McDonough, *Cradle to Cradle: Remaking the Way We Make Things,* North Point Press, 2002.
http://www.mcdonough.com
http://www.amazon.com/exec/obidos/tg/detail/-
/0865475873/102-4182705-8113758?v=glance
http://www.ewire.com/display.cfm/Wire_ID/2025
http://www.designboom.com/eng/funclub/cradle.html
http://www.housingzone.com/topics/pb/management/
pb02aa022f.asp

Green plus green makes green.
Green Building Forum
http://www.housingzone.com/forums/green/index.as

Sustainable Business Investing
http://www.sustainablebusiness.com/progressiveinvestor/index.cfm

Care2Make a Difference - Green Business
http://www.care2.com/channels/ecoinfo/green_business

Feeding two birds with one scone . . .
Social Venture Network
http://www.svn.org/

Global Exchange
http://www.globalexchange.org/

Chapter Six. Revitalize the Body Politic.

Our growing incarcenoma.
Incarceration is not an equal opportunity punishment
http://www.prisonsucks.com/

Crime and incarceration around the world:
http://www.prisonpolicy.org/prisonindex/globalincarceration.shtml

Corporate warriors and soldiers of misfortune.
P. W. Singer, Corporate Warriors: The Rise of the Privatized
Military Industry. Cornell University Press, 2003.
http://www.cornellpress.cornell.edu/cup_catalog.

The Multinational Monitor
http://multinationalmonitor.org/

The F-Word.
Laurence Britt's article, Fascism Anyone?
Appeared in Free Inquiry Magazine, published
by the Council for Secular Humanism.
http://www.secularhumanism.org/library/fi/britt_23_2.htm

Democracy from the ground up topples Humpty Dumpty.
Bringing Down a Dictator
http://www.pbs.org/weta/dicta

Exercise your rights . . .
True Majority, Jerry Cohen of Ben and Jerry
http://action.truemajority.org/register/

MoveOn, One of the most effective grassroots organizations
http://www.moveon.org/front/
http://www.pbs.org/weta/dictator/

. . . and do free press presses . . .
http://www.mediafordemocracy.us/mfd/homepage.html

Get your news online, and put your money where your mouse is . . .
Truth Out
http://www.truthout.org

Op Ed News
http://www.opednews.com/

AlterNet
http://www.alternet.org/

Chapter Seven. Don't Get Even, Get Odd.

Addicted to War . . .
Joel Andreas, *Addicted to War*, Frank Dorrel, 2002, 2003.
http://www.addictedtowar.com

Forgive . . . for goodness sake.
Fred Luskin, *Forgive for Good: A Proven Prescription for Health and Happiness*, Harper Collins, 2002.
http://www.stanford.edu/~alexsox/forgiveness.htm

Two birds in the hand . . .
Lynne Twist, *The Soul of Money, Transforming Your Relationship with Money and Life*, W. W. Norton & Company, 2003.
http://www.soulofmoney.org/
http://www.pachamama.org/

Yes, folks there is a Million Clown March . . .
http://www.clownarchy.org/million_clowns.htm

About Steve Bhaerman

S teve Bhaerman is an internationally known author, humorist, and workshop leader. For the past 18 years, he has written and performed as Swami Beyondananda, the "Cosmic Comic." Swami's comedy has been called "irreverently uplifting" and has been described both as "comedy disguised as wisdom" and "wisdom disguised as comedy."

As the Swami, Steve is the author of three previous books, *Driving Your Own Karma, When You See a Sacred Cow, Milk It For All It's Worth*, and *Duck Soup for the Soul*. Swami's nationally syndicated spoof advice column, Ask the Swami — along with his comedy performances — have found a wide and appreciative audience.

In his "past life" (before Swami), Steve started an alternative high school in Washington, D.C. and co-authored a book about his experiences, *No Particular Place to Go: Making of a Free High School*. A political science major, he later taught history to autoworkers at Wayne State University in Detroit as part of the Weekend College.

In 1980, Steve co-founded Pathways Magazine in Ann Arbor, Michigan, one of the first publications bringing together holistic health, personal growth, spirituality, and politics. The Swami was a regular comedy feature in Pathways, and helped launch Steve's career as the cosmic comic. Having spent his deformative years in Brooklyn, Steve earned a black belt in Borscht Belt, and has won numerous Irony-man competitions. He currently resides in Santa Rosa, California with his wife Trudy.

To find out more about booking the Swami for events,
or ordering products, go to his website at
www.wakeuplaughing.com

About Brian Narelle

Brian Narelle began drawing cartoons at the age of eight and no one has been able to stop him since. Though he has taken divergent paths that include starring in John Carpenter's cult classic *Dark Star,* creating the original San Diego Chicken, working on the Korty/Lucas feature *Twice Upon A Time* as Supervising Animator and Sequence Director, authoring *Living In Vertical Time* (wherein he started a church that worships a donkey named Murray!), writing and performing in numerous award-winning educational films and children's TV: including PBS specials, *Sesame Street* and the Discovery Channel's *Bingo & Molly,* and writing the screenplay for the Annie Award-winning animated short *Hubert's Brain,* he has persisted in doodling on napkins whenever possible. His cartoons have appeared in books, magazines, comics, newsletters, and the web - just about everywhere except the side of subway cars.

Narelle defines cartooning as "truth graphically portrayed with humor using the least possible amount of ink." His pen is ever ready to bring humor and clarity to bear on any situation. He can be reached at bnarelle@earthlink.net.

Visit www.narellecreative.com.

Printed in the United States
36498LVS00007B/33

9 780975 598306